American Revision Committee

Anglo-American Bible revision

American Revision Committee

Anglo-American Bible revision

ISBN/EAN: 9783337170035

Printed in Europe, USA, Canada, Australia, Japan

Cover: Foto ©Lupo / pixelio.de

More available books at **www.hansebooks.com**

ANGLO-AMERICAN

BIBLE REVISION.

BY

MEMBERS OF THE AMERICAN REVISION COMMITTEE.

PRINTED FOR PRIVATE CIRCULATION.

NEW YORK:
Nos. 42 AND 44 BIBLE HOUSE.
1879.

Copyright, by the AMERICAN SUNDAY-SCHOOL UNION, 1879.

PREFATORY NOTE.

THESE essays on the various aspects of the Anglo-American Bible revision now going on, are issued by the American Revision Committee as an explanatory statement to the friends and patrons of the cause, with the distinct understanding that suggestions and statements in regard to any particular changes to be made, express only the individual opinions of the writer, but not the final conclusions of the two Committees, who have not yet finished their work.

PHILIP SCHAFF,

NEW YORK, *March, 1879.*   *In behalf of the Committee.*

CONTENTS.

	PAGE
LIST OF ENGLISH REVISERS	7–10
LIST OF AMERICAN REVISERS	11–13

ANGLO-AMERICAN BIBLE REVISION:

INTRODUCTORY STATEMENT.
Philip Schaff. 14

THE AUTHORIZED VERSION AND ENGLISH VERSIONS ON WHICH IT IS BASED.
Chas. P. Krauth. 22

THE ENGLISH BIBLE AS A CLASSIC.
T. W. Chambers. 37

REASONS FOR A NEW REVISION.
Theo. D. Woolsey. 43

THE CURRENT VERSION AND PRESENT NEEDS.
G. Emlen Hare. 48

THE HEBREW TEXT OF THE OLD TESTAMENT.
Howard Osgood. 53

HEBREW PHILOLOGY AND BIBLICAL SCIENCE.
W. Henry Green. 60

HELPS FOR TRANSLATING THE HEBREW SCRIPTURES AT THE TIME THE ANCIENT VERSION WAS MADE.
George E. Day. 72

INACCURACIES OF THE AUTHORIZED VERSION OF THE OLD TESTAMENT.
Joseph Packard. 80

THE NEW TESTAMENT TEXT.
Ezra Abbot. 86

PAGE

INACCURACIES OF THE AUTHORIZED VERSION IN RESPECT OF GRAMMAR AND EXEGESIS.
A. C. Kendrick. 99

TRUE CONSERVATISM IN RESPECT TO CHANGES IN THE ENGLISH AND GREEK TEXT.
Timothy Dwight. 113

THE GREEK VERB IN THE NEW TESTAMENT.
Matthew B. Riddle. 126

UNWARRANTED VERBAL DIFFERENCES AND AGREEMENTS IN THE ENGLISH VERSION.
J. Henry Thayer. 133

ARCHAISMS; OR, OBSOLETE AND UNUSUAL WORDS AND PHRASES IN THE ENGLISH BIBLE.
Howard Crosby. 144

THE PROPER NAMES OF THE BIBLE.
Chas. A. Aiken. 151

THE USE OF ITALICS IN THE ENGLISH BIBLE.
Thomas Chase. 157

PARAGRAPHS, CHAPTERS, AND VERSES OF THE BIBLE.
James Strong. 166

REVISION OF THE SCRIPTURES AND CHURCH AUTHORITY.
Alfred Lee. 170

GENERAL INDEX . . . . . } *S. Austin Allibone.* { 181
INDEX OF TEXTS. 189

LIST OF REVISERS.

I. ENGLISH REVISION COMMITTEE.

(1) OLD TESTAMENT COMPANY.

The Right Rev. EDWARD HAROLD BROWNE, D.D., Bishop of Winchester (Chairman), Farnham Castle, Surrey.
The Right Rev. Lord ARTHUR CHARLES HERVEY, D.D., Bishop of Bath and Wells, Palace, Wells, Somerset.
The Right Rev. ALFRED OLLIVANT, D.D., Bishop of Llandaff, Bishop's Court, Llandaff.
The Very Rev. ROBERT PAYNE SMITH, D.D., Dean of Canterbury, Deanery, Canterbury.
The Ven. BENJAMIN HARRISON, M.A., Archdeacon of Maidstone, Canon of Canterbury, Canterbury.
The Rev. WILLIAM LINDSAY ALEXANDER, D.D., Professor of Theology, Congregational Church Hall, Edinburgh.
ROBERT L. BENSLY, Esq., Fellow and Hebrew Lecturer, Gonville and Caius College, Cambridge.
The Rev. JOHN BIRRELL, Professor of Oriental Languages, St. Andrew's, Scotland.
FRANK CHANCE, Esq., M.D., Burleigh House, Sydenham Hill, London.
THOMAS CHENERY, Esq., Reform Club, London, S. W.
The Rev. T. K. CHEYNE, Fellow and Hebrew Lecturer, Balliol College, Oxford.
The Rev. A. B. DAVIDSON, D.D., Professor of Hebrew, Free Church College, Edinburgh.
The Rev. GEORGE DOUGLAS, D.D., Professor of Hebrew and Principal of Free Church College, Glasgow.
S. R. DRIVER, Esq., Tutor of New College, Oxford.
The Rev. C. J. ELIOTT, Winkfield Vicarage, Windsor.

The Rev. Frederick Field, D.D., Carlton Terrace, Heigham, Norwich.

The Rev. John Dury Geden, Professor of Hebrew, Wesleyan College, Didsbury, Manchester.

The Rev. Christian D. Ginsburg, LL.D., Wokingham, Berks.

The Rev. Frederick William Gotch, D.D., Principal of the Baptist College, Bristol.

The Rev. William Kay, D.D., Great Leghs' Rectory, Chelmsford.

The Rev. Stanley Leathes, B.D., Professor of Hebrew, King's College, London.

The Rev. John Rawson Lumby, B.D., Fellow of St. Catharine's College, Cambridge.

The Rev. John James Stewart Perowne, D.D., Dean of Peterborough.

The Rev. A. H. Sayce, Fellow and Tutor of Queen's College, Oxford.

The Rev. William Robertson Smith, Professor of Hebrew, Free Church College, Aberdeen.

William Wright, Professor of Arabic, Cambridge.

William Aldis Wright, Esq. (Secretary), Bursar of Trinity College, Cambridge.

O. T. Company, 27.

Note.—The English Old Testament Company has lost, by death, the Right Rev. Dr. Connop Thirlwall, Bishop of St. David's, d. 27 July, 1875; the Ven. Henry John Rose, Archdeacon of Bedford, d. 31 January, 1873; the Rev. William Selwyn, D.D., Canon of Ely, d. 24 April, 1875; the Rev. Dr. Patrick Fairbairn, Principal of the Free Church College, Glasgow, d. 6 August, 1874; Professors McGill, d. 16 March, 1871; Weir, 27 July, 1876; and Davies, 19 July, 1875; and by resignation, the Right Rev. Dr. Christopher Wordsworth, Bishop of Lincoln; the Rev. John Jebb, Canon of Hereford, and the Rev. Edward Hayes Plumptre, D.D., Professor of N. T. Exegesis, King's College, London (resigned 17 March, 1874).

(2) New Testament Company.

The Right Rev. CHARLES JOHN ELLICOTT, D.D., Bishop of Gloucester and Bristol (Chairman), Palace, Gloucester.

The Right Rev. GEORGE MOBERLY, D.C.L., Bishop of Salisbury, Palace, Salisbury.

The Very Rev. EDWARD HENRY BICKERSTETH, D.D., Prolocutor, Dean of Lichfield, Deanery, Lichfield.

The Very Rev. ARTHUR PENRHYN STANLEY, D.D., Dean of Westminster, Deanery, Westminster.

The Very Rev. ROBERT SCOTT, D.D., Dean of Rochester, Deanery, Rochester.

The Very Rev. JOSEPH WILLIAMS BLAKESLEY, B.D., Dean of Lincoln, Deanery, Lincoln.

The Most Rev. RICHARD CHENEVIX TRENCH, D.D., Archbishop of Dublin, Palace, Dublin.

The Right Rev. CHARLES WORDSWORTH, D.C.L., Bishop of St. Andrew's, Bishopshall, St. Andrew's.

The Rev. JOSEPH ANGUS, D.D., President of the Baptist College, Regent's Park, London.

The Rev. DAVID BROWN, D.D., Principal of the Free Church College, Aberdeen.

The Rev. FENTON JOHN ANTHONY HORT, D.D., Fellow of Emmanuel College, Cambridge.

The Rev. WILLIAM GIBSON HUMPHRY, Vicarage, St. Martin's-in-the-Fields, London, W. C.

The Rev. BENJAMIN HALL KENNEDY, D.D., Canon of Ely and Regius Professor of Greek, The Elms, Cambridge.

The Ven. WILLIAM LEE, D.D., Archdeacon of Dublin, Dublin.

The Rev. JOSEPH BARBER LIGHTFOOT, D.D., Bishop of Durham.

The Rev. WILLIAM MILLIGAN, D.D., Professor of Divinity and Biblical Criticism, Aberdeen.

The Rev. WILLIAM F. MOULTON, D.D., Master of The Leys School, Cambridge.

The Rev. SAMUEL NEWTH, D.D., Principal of New College, Hampstead, London.

The Ven. EDWIN PALMER, D.D., Archdeacon of Oxford, Christ Church, Oxford.

The Rev. ALEXANDER ROBERTS, D.D., Professor of Humanity, St. Andrew's.

The Rev. FREDERICK HENRY AMBROSE SCRIVENER, LL.D., Prebendary, Hendon Vicarage, London, N. W.

The Rev. GEORGE VANCE SMITH, D.D., Parade, Carmarthen.

The Rev. CHARLES JOHN VAUGHAN, D.D., Master of the Temple, The Temple, London, E. C.

The Rev. BROOKE FOSS WESTCOTT, D.D., Canon of Peterborough and Regius Professor of Divinity, Trinity College, Cambridge.

The Rev. J. TROUTBECK (Secretary), Dean's Yard, Westminster.

N. T. Company, 25.
Active members in both Companies, 52.

NOTE.—The English New Testament Company has lost, by death, the Right Rev. Dr. SAMUEL WILBERFORCE, Bishop of Winchester, d. 1873; the Very Rev. Dr. HENRY ALFORD, Dean of Canterbury, d. 1871; the Rev. Dr. JOHN EADIE, Professor of Biblical Literature in the United Presbyterian Church, Glasgow, d. 1876; and Mr. SAMUEL PRIDEAUX TREGELLES, LL.D. (who was prevented by ill health from taking any part in the work), d. 1875; and by resignation, the Rev. Dr. CHARLES MERIVALE, Dean of Ely.

(The Rev. F. C. COOK, Canon of Exeter, the Rev. Dr. E. B. PUSEY, who were asked to join the O. T. Company, and the Rev. Dr. J. H. NEWMAN, who was asked to join the N. T. Company, declined to serve.)

II. AMERICAN REVISION COMMITTEE.

GENERAL OFFICERS OF THE COMMITTEE.
PHILIP SCHAFF, D.D., LL.D., President.
GEORGE E. DAY, D.D., Secretary.

(1) OLD TESTAMENT COMPANY.

Professor WM. HENRY GREEN, D.D., LL.D. (Chairman), Theological Seminary, Princeton, N. J.

Professor GEORGE E. DAY, D.D. (Secretary), Divinity School of Yale College, New Haven, Conn.

Professor CHARLES A. AIKEN, D.D., Theological Seminary, Princeton, N. J.

The Rev. T. W. CHAMBERS, D.D., Collegiate Reformed Dutch Church, N. Y.

Professor THOMAS J. CONANT, D.D., Brooklyn, N. Y.

Professor JOHN DE WITT, D.D., Theological Seminary, New Brunswick, N. J.

Professor GEORGE EMLEN HARE, D.D., LL.D., Divinity School, Philadelphia.

Professor CHARLES P. KRAUTH, D.D., LL.D., Vice-Provost of the University of Pennsylvania, Philadelphia.

Professor CHARLES M. MEAD, D.D., Theological Seminary, Andover, Mass.

Professor HOWARD OSGOOD, D.D., Theological Seminary, Rochester, N. Y.

Professor JOSEPH PACKARD, D.D., Theological Seminary, Alexandria, Va.

Professor CALVIN E. STOWE, D.D., Hartford, Conn.

Professor JAMES STRONG, S.T.D., Theological Seminary, Madison, N. J.

Professor C. V. A. VAN DYCK, D.D., M.D., Beirût, Syria. (Advisory Member on questions of Arabic).

O. T. Company, 14.

NOTE.—The American Old Testament Company has lost by death, TAYLER LEWIS, LL.D., Professor Emeritus of Greek and Hebrew, Union College, Schenectady, N. Y., d. 1877.

(2) New Testament Company.

Ex-President T. D. Woolsey, D.D., LL.D. (Chairman), New Haven, Conn.

Professor J. Henry Thayer, D.D. (Secretary), Theological Seminary, Andover, Mass.

Professor Ezra Abbot, D.D., LL.D., Divinity School, Harvard University, Cambridge, Mass.

The Rev. J. K. Burr, D.D., Trenton, New Jersey.

President Thomas Chase, LL.D., Haverford College, Pa.

Chancellor Howard Crosby, D.D., LL.D., New York University, New York.

Professor Timothy Dwight, D.D., Divinity School of Yale College, New Haven, Conn.

Professor A. C. Kendrick, D.D., LL.D., University of Rochester, Rochester, N. Y.

The Right Rev. Alfred Lee, D.D., Bishop of the Diocese of Delaware.

Professor Matthew B. Riddle, D.D., Theological Seminary, Hartford, Conn.

Professor Philip Schaff, D.D., LL.D., Union Theological Seminary, New York.

Professor Charles Short, LL.D., Columbia College, N.Y.

The Rev. E. A. Washburn, D.D., Calvary Church, N. Y.

N. T. Company, 13.

In both Companies, 27.

Note.—The American New Testament Company has lost by death, James Hadley, LL.D., Professor of Greek, Yale College, Conn. (who attended the first session), d. 1872; Professor Henry Boynton Smith, D.D., LL.D., Union Theological Seminary, New York (who attended one session, and resigned, from ill health), d. 1877; Professor Horatio B. Hackett, D.D., LL.D., Theological Seminary, Rochester, N. Y., d. 1876; and Professor Charles Hodge, D.D. LL.D., Theological Seminary, Princeton, N. J. (who never attended the meetings, but corresponded with the Committee), d. 1878; and by resignation, Rev. G. R. Crooks, D.D., New York, and Rev. W. F. Warren, D.D., Boston (who accepted the original appointment, but found it impossible to attend).

(A number of Bishops of the Protestant Episcopal Church, and Professors of sacred learning, who had been invited to join the American Committee at its first organization in 1871, declined, from want of time, or other reasons, but expressed interest in the work, and confidence in its success.)

MEMBERS OF THE FINANCE COMMITTEE CO-OPERATING WITH THE AMERICAN BIBLE REVISION COMMITTEE.

Hon. NATHAN BISHOP, LL.D., Chairman.
ANDREW L. TAYLOR, Esq., Treasurer

Rev. WILLIAM ADAMS, D.D., LL.D.
A. S. BARNES, Esq.
WILLIAM A. CAULDWELL, Esq.
Rev. H. DYER, D.D.
Hon. E. L. FANCHER, LL.D.
MORRIS K. JESSUP, Esq.
HOWARD POTTER, Esq.
Rev. RICHARD S. STORRS, D.D., LL.D.
JNO. B. TREVOR, Esq.
NORMAN WHITE, Esq.
Rev. THOMAS D. ANDERSON, D.D.
JAMES M. BROWN, Esq.
Hon. WM. E. DODGE.
JOHN ELLIOT, Esq.
JOHN C. HAVEMEYER, Esq.
Rev. HENRY C. POTTER, D.D., LL.D.
ELLIOTT F. SHEPARD, Esq.
CHARLES TRACY, Esq.
ROSWELL SMITH, Esq.
F. S. WINSTON, Esq.
S. D. WARREN, Esq.

THE ANGLO-AMERICAN BIBLE REVISION.

INTRODUCTORY STATEMENT.

BY PHILIP SCHAFF, D.D., LL.D.,
Professor of Sacred Literature, Union Theological Seminary, New York.

I. ORIGIN AND ORGANIZATION.—The Anglo-American Bible Revision movement now in progress is the first *inter-national* and *inter-denominational* effort in the history of the translation of the Bible. The present and the older authorized English versions for public use in churches proceeded from the undivided national Church of England, before the other evangelical denominations were organized, and before the American people had an independent existence.

The new revision took its origin, very properly, in the Convocation of Canterbury (the cradle of Anglo-Saxon Christendom), May 6, 1870, by the appointment of a Committee of eminent Biblical scholars and dignitaries of the Church of England, with power to revise, for public use, the authorized English version of 1611, and to associate with them representative Biblical scholars of other Christian denominations using that version.

The English Committee is divided into two Companies, one for the Old Testament and one for the New, and holds regular meetings in the historic Jerusalem Chamber (sometimes in the Chapter Library) in the Deanery of Westminster, London.

The American Committee was organized in 1871, by invitation, and with the approval, of the British Revisers, and began active work in October, 1872. It is likewise selected from different denominations, and divided into two Companies, which meet once a month, for several days, in their own rooms in the Bible House, at New

York, but the American Bible Society has no part or responsibility in this enterprise, and can have none within the limits of its present constitution.

The British and American Committees are virtually one organization, with the same principles and objects, and in constant correspondence with each other. They do not intend to issue two separate and distinct revisions, but one and the same revision for both nations.

II. COMPOSITION.—The two Committees embrace at present 79 active members (52 in England and 27 in America). Besides, the English Committee lost by death and resignation 15, the American Committee 7, members. Adding these, the whole number of scholars who at any time have been connected with this work, amounts to 101. Among these are many of the best Biblical scholars and commentators of the leading Protestant denominations in Great Britain and the United States. Not a few of them are well known by their works, in Europe and America. We need only refer to the list at the beginning of this volume. The American members are nearly all Professors of Hebrew or Greek exegesis in the principal theological institutions of the Eastern States, and have been selected with regard to competency and reputation for Biblical scholarship, denominational connection, and local convenience or easy reach of New York, where they meet every month. Several distinguished divines in the far West or South, whose coöperation would have been very desirable had, of necessity, to be omitted; others, from want of time, or other reasons, declined to coöperate.

III. THE OBJECT of this Anglo-American enterprise is to adapt King James's version to the present state of the English language, without changing the idiom and vocabulary, and to the present standard of Biblical scholarship, which has made very great advances since 1611, especially during the last thirty years, in textual criticism, Greek and Hebrew philology, in Biblical geography and archæology.

It is not the intention to furnish a new *version* (which is not needed, and would not succeed), but a conservative *revision* of the received version, so deservedly esteemed as far as the English language extends. The new Bible is to read like the old, and the sacred associations connected with it are not to be disturbed; but within these limits all necessary and desirable corrections and improvements on which the best scholars are agreed will be introduced: a good version is to be made better; a clear and accurate version clearer and more accurate; the oldest and purest text is to be followed; errors, obscurities, and inconsistencies are to be removed; uniformity in rendering Hebrew and Greek words and proper names to be sought. In one word, the revision is to give, in idiomatic English, the nearest possible equivalent for the original Word of God as it came from the inspired organs of the Holy Spirit. It aims to be the best version possible in the nineteenth century, as King James's version was the best which could be made in the seventeenth century.

IV. THE PRINCIPLES of the revision, as adopted at the outset by both Committees, are the following:—

"1. To introduce as few alterations as possible into the text of the authorized version consistently with faithfulness.

(Faithfulness to the original, which is the first duty of a translator, requires a great many changes, though mostly of an unessential character.)

"2. To limit, as far as possible, the expression of such alterations to the language of the authorized or earlier versions.

(So far, only one new word has been introduced in the New Testament.)

"3. Each Company to go twice over the portion to be revised, once provisionally, the second time finally.

"4. That the text to be adopted be that for which the evidence is decidedly preponderating; and that when the text so adopted differs from that from which the authorized version was made, the alteration be indicated in the margin.

(The Hebrew text followed is the Masoretic, which presents few variations. The text of the New Testament is taken from the oldest and best uncial MSS., the oldest versions, and patristic quotations; while the received text from which King James's version was made, is derived from comparatively late mediæval MSS.)

"5. To make or retain no change in the text, on the second final revision by each Company, except two-thirds of those present approve of the same; but on the first revision to decide by simple majorities.

"6. In every case of proposed alteration that may have given rise to discussion, to defer the voting thereon till the next meeting, whensoever the same shall be required by one-third of those present at the meeting, such intended vote to be announced in the notice for the next meeting.

"7. To revise the headings of chapters, pages, paragraphs, italics, and punctuation.

"8. To refer, on the part of each Company, when considered desirable, to divines, scholars, and literary men, whether at home or abroad, for their opinions."

If these principles are faithfully carried out (as they have been thus far), the people need not apprehend any dangerous innovations. No article of faith, no moral precept, will be disturbed, no sectarian views will be introduced. The revision will so nearly resemble the present version, that the mass of readers and hearers will scarcely perceive the difference; while a careful comparison will show slight improvements in every chapter and almost in every verse. The only serious difficulty may arise from a change of the text in a few instances where the overwhelming evidence of the oldest manuscripts makes a change necessary; and perhaps also from the omission of italics, the metrical arrangement of poetry and the sectional of prose, and from new headings of chapters, which, however, are no part of the Word of God, and may be handled with greater freedom.

V. MODE OF OPERATION.—The English Companies transmit, from time to time, confidential copies of their revision to the American Companies; the American Companies send the results of their labors to the British Companies, likewise in strict confidence. Then follows a second revision on the part of both Committees, with a view to harmonize the two revisions, and the results of the second revision are transmitted in like manner.

If any differences should remain, after a final vote, they will be indicated in an appendix or preface. Happily, they will be few and unessential as compared with the large number of improvements already adopted by both Committees.

The work is not distributed among sub-committees, as was the case with the Revisers of King James, but the whole Old Testament Company goes carefully through all the books of the Old Testament, the New

Testament Company through those of the New; and in this way greater harmony and consistency will be secured than was possible under the other system.

The revision has been wisely carried on without publicity, and the actual results of their labors are not yet made known. Any public statements, therefore, of particular changes are wholly unauthorized and premature. The Committees, by publishing parts of their work before a final revision, would become entangled in controversy and embarrassed in their progress.

When the revision is thoroughly matured, it will be given to the public, as the joint work of both Committees, by the University Presses of Oxford and Cambridge, which publish the best and cheapest editions of the Bible in England, and will insure the utmost accuracy in typography. When adopted by the Churches and Bible Societies of the two countries, the revised English Bible will become public property, like King James's version.

VI. EXPENSES.—The labor of the Revisers in both countries is given without compensation. The necessary expenses for travelling, printing, etc., of the British Committee, are paid by the University Presses; those of the American Committee, by voluntary contributions of liberal friends, under the direction of an auxiliary Committee of Finance.

VII. PROGRESS AND PROBABLE RESULT.—It was calculated at the beginning of the work that the revision could be completed in ten years of uninterrupted labor. It may take about two years more. At this time (December, 1878) the two New Testament Companies have finished the first and a part of the second revision (the English Company being several months ahead of the American); the Old Testament Companies have done more than half, perhaps two-thirds, of their work. It is probable that the revised New Testament, at least, possibly also parts of the Old Testament, will be published in 1880, just five hundred years after John Wycliffe finished the first complete version of the Holy Scriptures in the English language.

After they have finished their labors the two Committees will disband. It will then be for the Churches and Bible Societies to take up the Revision, and to decide whether it shall take the place of King James's Version, or at least be used alongside with it, in public worship. It is not expected, of course, that the old version, which is so deeply imbedded in our religious literature, will ever go entirely out of use, certainly not for a long time to come.

The Revision will, no doubt, be opposed, like everything new, and will have to pass through a severe ordeal of criticism. Many will condemn it as too radical, others as too conservative, but it will be found ultimately to occupy the sound medium between the two opposite extremes. The Churches will have either to adopt this Anglo-American Bible, or to dismiss an œcumenical revision for an indefinite number of years. In the one case we shall retain the bond of inter-denominational and inter-national union in a common Bible; in the other, the irrepressible task of correcting King James's Version will be carried on more zealously than ever by unauthorized individuals, and by sectarian enterprise, which will increase the difficulty by multiplying confusion and division.

But we never had the least fear of the final result. There never has been such a truly providential combination of favorable circumstances, and of able and sound Biblical scholars from all the evangelical Churches of the two great nations speaking the English language, for such a holy work of our common Christianity, as is presented in the Anglo-American Bible Revision Committees. This providential juncture, the remarkable harmony of the Revisers in the prosecution of their work, and the growing desire of the Churches for a timely improvement and rejuvenation of our venerable English Version, justify the expectation of a speedy and general adoption of the new Revision in Great Britain and America.

THE OLDER ENGLISH AND THE AUTHORIZED VERSIONS.

BY CHARLES P. KRAUTH, S.T.D., LL.D.,
Vice-Provost of the University of Pennsylvania.

I. CHRISTIANITY ENTERED BRITAIN in the second century, prevailed in the third, waned with the passing away of the Roman power, went down before the march of the Pagan invaders, rose again in the sixth century, and was again triumphant before the close of the seventh. Saxon paraphrases and versions of the Psalter, of the Gospels, and of other parts of Holy Scripture, were early made from the Latin. The Danish inroads checked the work of Saxon translation, and the Norman Conquest rendered it useless.

II. WYCLIFFE AND THE REFORMATION.—In the fourteenth century arose Wycliffe (1324–1384). Called to the work of Reformation in faith and life, he saw, with the divine instincts of his mission, that nothing but the true rule of faith and life could remove the evil and restore the good, and that the restoration would be permanent only in the degree to which every estate of the Church should be enabled, by possession of the rule, to apply and guard its teachings. He appealed to the Word, and to sustain his appeal translated the Word. He appealed to the people, and put into their hands the book divinely given to shape their convictions. The translation of the Scriptures as a whole into English first came from his hands or under his supervision. It was finished in the last quarter of the fourteenth century. It was made from the Vulgate. Even had Wycliffe been a Greek and Hebrew scholar, it is doubtful whether he could have secured texts of the sacred originals from which to translate. That he translated the version universally received in the Western Church, quoted by her fathers, read, and sung, and preached from, in her services, and that he rendered it with a severe closeness approaching servility, would help to remove prejudice, and to avert or soften the suspicion that he was adapting Scripture to his own ends, against the Roman hierarchy. Like Luther, Wycliffe drew to him co-workers in his translation; like Luther he suffered from plagiarists of his work; like Luther he saw his work eagerly circulated, bitterly opposed, and triumphant over opposition; like Luther he escaped the stake, with which he was threatened; like Luther his enemies sought to wreak upon his bones the malice which survived his death, but there was no Charles the Fifth to respond, "I war with the living, not with the dead." The Council of Constance ordered the dishonoring of Wycliffe's remains; Pope Martin the Fifth, in the cold blood of a delay of thirteen years, commanded the execution of the order; the Bishop of Lincoln, an apostate adherent of Wycliffe, obeyed it. The bones were burned, and winds and waves swept them into an " emblem of his doctrine, which is now dispersed all the world over." Wycliffe was the dayspring of the coming noontide of divine light.

III. PAPER AND PRINTING.—Two material aids were maturing, to bear part in the grand revolution which was approaching. Paper made from rags began in the thirteenth century to take the place of parchment; printing from movable type, in the fifteenth, began the unequal contest with the pen. Paper and printing were to be in the struggle of thought what powder and firearms had become in the battle-field. Had it not been for the new arts which intellectualize man, the new arts which were tributary to war would only have made the domain of brute force complete and final. The lamp-black and oil were to neutralize the nitre, and charcoal, and sulphur.

IV. Tyndale's Translation.—The illustrious Englishman who was to be the father of the era to come, in the translation of scripture into his vernacular, was William Tyndale. He was "to cause the boy who driveth the plow to know more of the Scriptures" than had been known by those who pretended to be divines. It is said that Tyndale met Luther at Wittenberg; it is certain that he met Luther in Luther's works, and that whether by personal or by spiritual contact, or by both, he drew the inspiration of a Biblical translator from the greatest of translators. Luther was Tyndale's exemplar and his master, not as the master of a slave, but as the master of a noble pupil. It is a legend that at Wittenberg Tyndale completed his translation, assisted by Roye, 1526. Using all the aids of the time, as fully as his harassed condition allowed, Tyndale used most of all the best of all, Luther's translations as they appeared. He followed Luther in the order in which his work appeared: the New Testament, the Pentateuch, Jonah. Tyndale's own final revision of his New Testament was finished 1534. From the prison in which his last hours were spent in adapting his work to the humblest of the people, he was taken forth, strangled, and burned to ashes. It is no extravagance to say that to him our English Bible owes more than to all the other laborers. His name will forever stand in the roll of the supreme benefactors of the race.

V. COVERDALE'S TRANSLATION.—Another wave of the great tide is sweeping on, before the first is wholly spent upon the shore. Tyndale was burned 1536. Coverdale, who is said to have aided Tyndale in his work at Hamburg, 1529, put forth a complete translation of the Bible in 1535, marking in the dedication to the king the change that was going on in England. Coverdale had neither the creative power nor Biblical learning of Tyndale. His translation bears internal evidence on every page that it was not made from the originals. It shows no acquaintance on the part of the translator with either Hebrew or Greek; it follows closely the translations it translates, and fully corroborates the statement of the title-page that it is "out of Douche [German] and Latyn," and the honest and explicit account of Coverdale himself, that it was "translated out of fyve sundry interpreters," "not onely in Latyn, but also of the Douche [German] interpreters." He says, with truth: "Lowly and faythfully have I followed myne interpreters;" he followed even their typographical errors, and sometimes transfers a word with an English sound without translating it. The Latin interpreters of the five are the Vulgate, and probably Erasmus and Pagninus; the German are Luther, and the Zurich Version, in part by Leo Juda (of the unchanged text previous to 1534). Tyndale's labors he has largely appropriated without acknowledgment. Coverdale's New Testament is Tyndale's, altered at times to correspond especially with the German, whose meaning Coverdale has not unfrequently mistaken. But Coverdale has introduced from his interpreters many felicities which linger still in the Authorized Version. The Coverdale Bible was submitted by Henry VIII. to the Bishops, was approved, and ordered to be placed in the churches. But before the order could be executed Henry was absorbed anew in one of those loves, not worthy of so sacred a name, which dictated his policy in Church and State, and his zeal for the Scriptures abated in proportion. The Bible, nevertheless, was tolerated, but the new dedication transferred to "the dearest just wife, and most virtuous princess, Queen Jane," what had been assigned, with the same epithets, in the first, to Queen Anne.

VI. MATTHEW'S BIBLE.—An ineffectual attempt was now made by Cranmer for a revision, to be made in conjunction with learned bishops and others. Soon after, what is called the Matthew's Bible appeared, 1537. It is a combination of the labors of Tyndale (partly posthumous) and of Coverdale, revised, and published under the assumed name of Matthew, by John Rogers, the friend of Tyndale. It was sent to Crumwell, and through his influence received the approval of that same royal authority which had helped to hunt its chief author to the death.

The principle of the free reading and circulation of the Holy Scriptures was coming to be generally accepted. As it became a settled conviction that the Scriptures of right belonged to the people, room was left for a more careful searching into the character of the particular translations. Fault was found with the Tyndale-Matthew's Bible, mainly because of its Prologues and Notes. The "Great Bible" appeared 1539, without these additions. It was edited by Coverdale, and printed at Paris, by permission of Francis I.

VII. THE GREAT BIBLE is a revision, very imperfectly made, of the Tyndale-Matthew's Bible. What is new is mainly drawn from Munster's Latin translation of the

Old Testament (1534–35). The inspiration and material for English revision came almost entirely from the Continent; England did not have an independent Biblical scholar of the highest order in the sixteenth century. The Great Bible inserts in smaller type, at their places, the peculiar renderings of the Vulgate. In general it is marked by the features of conservatism endeavoring to harmonize with reformation. The Inquisition set itself against the civil power, and in spite of the permission granted by the King of France, the Bibles were seized and most of them burned. A few, however, were saved and completed in London 1539. Taverner's Bible (1539), is also a hasty revision of Tyndale, but retains the marginal notes and increases their number. In 1540 appeared the CRANMER BIBLE, which is a revision in part of the Great Bible of the previous year. It takes its name from the Archbishop's prologue, and the official responsibility of the changes rests with him.

VIII. HENRY VIII. AND THE BIBLE.—In various accidents Henry VIII. seemed to be a Protestant; in substance he never ceased to be a Romanist; his opposition to the Pope was the result of the opposition of the Pope to him. A compliant Papacy might have kept Henry the most rigorous Papist of his age. His policy was a see-saw of self-will. The beauty of Catharine Howard cost Crumwell his head. Soon after, three Protestants and three Papists were burned together, the former for asserting the doctrine of justification by faith, the latter for want of faith in the king's supremacy. The king saw to it that the Bible was circulated, and then piously burned men to death for believing it in any respect wherein it did not agree with the king's views. It was rather in spite of the dubious aid given by Henry, than in consequence of it, that God's Word was widely circulated and read.

IX. Coverdale and Rogers.—After the death of Henry VIII.(1547), Somerset, the Lord Protector, removed the restriction which had embarrassed the reading of the Scriptures. Coverdale was made Bishop of Exeter 1551, but was too poor to take possession. All things changed on the accession of Mary. Rogers, after his editorship of the Matthew's Bible, had been at Wittenberg, and legend affirms, " being skilled in the German language, took charge of a congregation there." He returned to England, only to lead the van of the martyrs of 1555. Coverdale, on the intercession of the King of Denmark, was allowed to take refuge in his dominion.

X. New Testament of 1557.—A translation of the New Testament appeared at Geneva 1557, probably by Whittingham, whose wife was Calvin's sister. It is largely, but not exclusively, a careful revision of Tyndale and Cranmer, with many proofs of the influence of Beza's labors. It has annotations; it marks by *italics* the words supplied, and for the first time in English has the division into verses, following the Greek of Stephanus, 1551.

XI. Geneva Bible 1560.—In 1560 the whole Bible, with annotations, appeared at Geneva. It is the work of a number of refugees on the Continent, and is really the first complete direct translation of the Bible into English from the originals throughout. It became the Bible of the people, and passed through more than a hundred editions. Coverdale, who had taken a prominent part in it, returned to England 1559, and died 1568, at the age of eighty-one, very poor in this world's goods, but very rich in the love of good men, and the approval of God.

XII. BISHOPS' BIBLE.—Under Elizabeth, the Cranmer Bible was in authority again. It was open, however, to many serious objections. One of the most vital, which largely contributed to the others, was, that it is not throughout made from the originals, that it is interpolated with what are confessedly translations of a translation, and that much of the revision is superficial, and some of it purely nominal. The Puritan origin of the Geneva Bible and the character of its notes prevented its universal acceptance. Parker, Archbishop of Canterbury, distributed the Cranmer Bible among the "able bishops and other learned men" for revision, subject to his own final decision. The result of their labor was published in 1568, and, after a somewhat completer revision, in 1572, and is known as the BISHOPS' BIBLE. It made a number of particular improvements and has brief notes, but was so devoid of elasticity, spontaneousness, and popular character, as to make it certain that its reception could, at most, be only provisional.

XIII. RHEIMS NEW TESTAMENT.—The Church of Rome was driven at last, in self defense, to publish an English translation of the New Testament. Rheims became the Geneva of the English Romanist refugees, and in 1582 they issued a translation of the New Testament "into English out of the authentical Latin," with annotations, exposures of the corruptions of other translations, and a great body of polemical matter. It is "out of" the Latin, as it claims to be, but its claim to be "into English" is at times more than doubtful. It exhibits traces of the influence of the Protestant renderings, but has given more than it has taken. Wycliffe and his mediæval co-workers can be distinctly traced in it. The Rheims, in an important class of religious terms, unmistakably influenced and benefitted the Authorized Version, and has carried over to it no few of the peculiarities of Wycliffe. To this is due the extraordinary fact that while there is hardly a seeming parallelism, and not a solitary demonstrable one, anywhere, between Wycliffe and Tyndale, the parallelisms are many between Wycliffe and the Authorized Version. This is another of the points of interest and beauty in that remarkable version, which, in its aggregations, stands almost unique as a miracle of providence and history, the symbol of England itself, whose greatness has so largely sprung from appropriating what others have produced and actualizing what others have dreamed.

XIV. KING JAMES'S BIBLE BEGUN.—When James I. came to the throne he found his subjects within the Church of England divided into Conformists and Puritans—those who were satisfied with the reformation already made, and those who wished a more radical one. The Puritans had high hopes of the King, and early laid their complaints before him. At the Hampton Conference, January 16, 1604, in which the two parties discussed the questions which divided them, a request came from Dr. Reynolds, a leader among the Puritans, for a new version of the Bible. The proposal was at first resisted by the churchly party, probably from a suspicion created by its source. The King pleased the Puritans by inclining to their request, and propitiated the Conformists by pronouncing the Geneva the worst of the English versions, made more intolerable by its untrue and traitorous notes. Prompt and wise measures were adopted for a new translation. Fifty-four learned men were appointed by the King for the work, who were also to secure the suggestions of all competent persons, that "our said translation may have the help and furtherance of all our principal learned men within this our kingdom." The attitude of the King, the removal of their first suspicions, and the merits of the case, brought about a hearty acquiescence on the part of those who had at first opposed the movement. His Majesty's instructions to the translators were these:—

INSTRUCTIONS TO THE TRANSLATORS.

"1. The ordinary Bible read in the Church, commonly called the Bishops' Bible, to be followed, and as little altered as the original will permit.

"2. The names of the prophets and the holy writers, with the other names in the text, to be retained, as near as may be, accordingly as they are vulgarly used.

"3. The old ecclesiastical words to be kept, as the word *church*, not to be translated *congregation*.

"4. When any word hath divers significations, that to be kept which hath been most commonly used by the most eminent fathers, being agreeable to the propriety of the place and the analogies of faith.

"5. The division of chapters to be altered either not at all or as little as may be, if necessity so require.

"6. No marginal notes at all to be affixed, but only for the explanation of the Hebrew or Greek words, which cannot, without some circumlocution, so briefly and fitly be expressed in the text.

"7. Such quotations of places to be marginally set down as shall serve for the fit reference of one Scripture to another.

"8. Every particular man of each company to take the same chapter or chapters; and, having translated or amended them severally by himself where he thinks good, all to meet together to confirm what they have done and agree for their part what shall stand.

"9. As any one company hath dispatched any one book in this manner, they shall send it to the rest, to be considered of seriously and judiciously; for his Majesty is very careful in this point.

"10. If any company, upon the review of the book so sent, shall doubt or differ upon any places, to send them word thereof, to note the places, and therewithall to send their reasons; to which if they consent not, the difference to be compounded at the general meeting, which is to be of the chief persons of each company, at the end of the work.

"11. When any place of special obscurity is doubted of, letters to be directed by authority to send to any learned in the land for his judgment in such a place.

"12. Letters to be sent from every bishop to the rest of his clergy, admonishing them of this translation in hand, and to move and charge as many as, being skillful in the tongues, have taken pains in that kind, to send their particular observations to the company, either at Westminster, Cambridge or Oxford, according as it was directed before in the King's letter to the archbishop.

"13. The directors in each company to be the Deans of Westminster and Chester, for Westminster, and the King's professors in Hebrew and Greek in the two universities.

"14. These translations to be used when they agree better with the text than the Bishops' Bible: Tyndale's, Coverdale's, Matthew's [Rogers's], Whitchurch's [Cranmer's], Geneva."

15. By a later rule "three or four of the most ancient and grave divines, in either of the Universities, not employed in translating, to be assigned to be overseers of the translation, for the better observation of the fourth rule."

The translators, probably forty-seven in all, were divided into six parties, two of which met in Oxford, two in Cambridge and two in Westminster. In their number were the greatest English scholars of the time. The learning of that age was almost exclusively in connection with theological interests. The rules prescribed by the King may be accepted as a guide to the mode in which the translators actually proceeded.

XV. KING JAMES'S BIBLE FINISHED.—The work commenced, probably, before the close of 1604: the New Version was issued 1611. It bore the title: "The Holy Bible, Conteyning the Old Testament, and the New: ¶ Newly Translated out of the Originall Tongues: and with the former translations diligently Compared and Revised." The second part of this statement is meant, in a certain sense, to define and qualify the first. The translation is new; but its newness is not that of a wholly independent work, but that of a revision, in which there has been a diligent comparison of the former English Translations, enumerated in the King's Instructions, the Bishops' Bible being laid as the general basis of the whole work. "Truly," say the translators, who were too great for the pretentiousness of a false independence, "we never thought, from the beginning, that we should need to make a new Translation, nor yet to make of a bad one a good one; but to make a good one better, or out of many good ones, one principal good one." Without this confession the Authorized Version would tell its own story. It is only necessary to compare it with the older versions, to see that with much that is original, with many characteristic beauties, in some of which no other translation approaches it, it is yet in the main a revision. Even its original beauties are often the mosaic of an exquisite combination of the fragments of the older. Comparing it with the English exemplars it follows, we must say it is not the fruit of their bloom, but the ripeness of their fruit.

The king, in endorsing the suggestion of Dr. Reynolds, had expressed the purpose that the new translation "should be ratified by royal authority, and adopted for exclusive use in all the churches." The title-page claims that the work is done by "his Maiesties special commandment," and is "appointed to be read in churches." It comes from the press of "Robert Barker, Printer to the King's most excellent Maiestie." Whatever may be the weight of civil authority implied in these statements, it is certain that the new version was left to win its way by its own merits purely, and that neither external nor moral coercion was employed in its behalf. The Epistles and Gospels from the Bishops' Bible were retained in the Prayer Book till the final revision in 1661; the Psalms from the Coverdale-Cranmer translation (not made from the Hebrew) are still retained.

XVI. EXCELLENCE OF KING JAMES'S VERSION.—The Bible of 1611 encountered prejudices and overcame them; it had rivals great in just claims and strong in possession, and it displaced them; it moved slowly that it might move surely; the Church of England lost many of her children, but they all took their mother's Bible with them, and taking that they were not wholly lost to her. It more and more melted indifference into cordial admiration, secured the enthusiastic approval of the cautious scholar, and won the artless love of the people. It has kindled into fervent praise men who were cold on every other theme. It glorified the tongue of the worshipper in glorifying God, and by the inspiration indwelling in it, and the inspiration it has imparted, has created English literature. Its most brilliant eulogies have come from those who, hating Protestantism, yet acknowledged the grandeur of this Book, which lives by that Protestantism of which it is the offspring, that Protestantism to which, world-wide, it gives life as one of its roots. When to him who has been caught in the snare of unbelief, or drawn by the lure of false belief, every other chord of the old music wakes only repugnant memories, its words have stolen in, too strong to be beaten back, too sweet to be renounced, once more the thunder of God's power, the pulsation of God's heart. Its faults have been hardly more than the foils of its beauties. It has so interwoven, by the artistic delicacy even of its mechanical transfers, the very idioms characteristic of the sacred tongues, that Hebraisms and Hellenisms need no comment to the English mind, but come as parts of its simplest, its noblest, its deepest thought and emotion. Its words are nearer to men than their own, and it gives articulation to groanings which but for it could not be uttered. It has lifted the living world to the solemn fixedness of those old heavenly thoughts and feelings, instead of dragging them by low, secular phrase out of their high and holy thrones, down to the dust of the shifting present, or leaving them dim and dreary behind the fog of pedantry. It has fought against the relentless tendency of time to change language, and has won all the great fields; words have dropped away or have deserted their meaning, as soldiers are lost even by the side which conquers; but the great body of the army of its ancient but not antiquated forms, among the sweetest and the highest speech beneath the voices of the upper world, remains intact and victorious. The swords of its armory may have gathered here and there a spot of rust, but their double edge has lost none of its keenness, and their broad surface little of its refulgence. It has made a new translation, as against something old and fading, impossible, for it is itself new, more fresh, more vital, more youthful than anything which has sought to supplant it. We need, and may have, a revision of it. Itself a revision of revisions, its own wonderful growth reveals the secret of the approach to perfection. But by very virtue of its grandly closing one era of struggle it opened another, for in human efforts all great endings are but great beginnings. A revision we may have, but a substitute, not now—it may be never. The accidents of our Authorized Version are open to change, but its substantial part is beyond it, until the English takes its place among the tongues that shall cease. The new revision will need little new English. Its best work will be to reduce the old English of the old Version to more perfect consistency with the text and with itself. That Version is now, and unchanged in essence will be, perhaps to the end of time, the mightiest bond—intellectual, social, and religious—of that vast body of nations which girdles the earth, and spreads far toward the poles, the nations to whom the English is the language of their hearts, and the English Bible the matchless standard of that language. So long as Christianity remains to them the light out of God, the English Bible will be cherished by millions as the dearest conservator of pure faith, the greatest power of holy life in the world.

THE ENGLISH BIBLE AS A CLASSIC.

BY TALBOT W. CHAMBERS, D.D.

Pastor of the Collegiate Reformed Dutch Church, New York.

KING JAMES'S BIBLE.—The merits of the Authorized Version, in point of fidelity to the original, are universally acknowledged. No other version, ancient or modern, surpasses it, save, perhaps, the Dutch, which was made subsequently, and profited by the labors of the English translators. But a version may be faithful without being elegant. It may be accurate without adequately representing the riches of the language in which it is made. The glory of the English Bible is that while it conveys the mind of the Spirit with great exactness, it does this in such a way that the book has become the highest existing standard of our noble tongue. Lord Macaulay calls it a stupendous work, which, if everything else in our language should perish, would alone suffice to show the whole extent of its beauty and power.

It is true that Mr. Hallam (*Literature of Europe*, II, 58) dissents from this view, and seems to regard it as a sort of superstition; but surely he is wrong. The praise of our version is not confined to men of any creed or class, but comes from nearly every eminent critic. Men who differ as widely in other matters as Addison, Swift, Coleridge, Matthew Arnold, both the Newmans, and Mr. Ruskin, yet agree on this point; and Mr. Huxley gave voice to a common opinion when he said, "It is written in the noblest and purest English, and abounds in exquisite beauties of mere literary form." It is, therefore, neither prejudice nor thoughtlessness which affirms this book to be the first of English classics. Indeed, its pages speak for themselves. In simplicity and strength, in the union of Saxon force and Latin dignity, in idiomatic ease and rhythmic flow, they have no superior.

STYLE OF THE VERSION.—Nor is it difficult to account for this. It is true that the style of writing which prevailed among men of letters in the reigns of Elizabeth and James I was not adapted to such composition. In many of these there was a strange fondness for alliteration, antithesis, fanciful analogies, pedantic allusions, and all sorts of conceits. Even Shakspeare has verbal quibbles which "make the judicious grieve." And when these are avoided, as in Bacon and Raleigh, there is a degree of stiffness, of inversion and occasionally of affectation, which would be an insuperable barrier in the way of popular acceptance and favor. The authors of our Bible seem to have been preserved from this error by a sort of providential preparation. In the course of the religious discussions which prevailed in England from the days of Wycliffe down there had grown up what Mr. Marsh calls "a consecrated diction," an assemblage of the best forms of expression suited to the communication of sacred truths. This dialect, if one may so style it, avoided equally the pedantry of the schools and the vulgarisms of the market-place. It never crawled upon the ground and never soared in the clouds. It was simple and direct, yet pure and dignified. It was intelligible to all classes, yet offensive to none. It seized as if by instinct the best elements of the vernacular speech, and moulded them into the most suitable grammatical forms; hence it is marked by the absence of book language or "inkhorn terms," and also of mere colloquial speech. The book was not the production of a single mind, but of many wise and good men, laboring through a series of years. The earliest and most influential of all was the martyr Tyndale, whose New Testament was issued in 1525. This was followed by Coverdale's Bible (1535), Rogers's (1537), Cranmer's (1539), the Genevan (1560), the Bishops' (1568). At last, in 1611, the final outcome of these years of toil appeared in our present Bible as it came from the hand of King James's translators. During all this period the process of revision went steadily forward, almost constantly gaining in every element of vigor and appropriateness.

AUTHORS OF KING JAMES'S VERSION.—The character of the authors had much to do with the perfection of their work. They were men of learning, judgment and piety, animated only by the sincere desire to render God's most holy Word accessible to all their countrymen. They toiled not for fame or pelf or any party interest, but for God's glory and the souls of men. They were in full and hearty sympathy with the book upon which they wrought. It was the guide of their lives, the arbiter of their differences, the charter of their hope for eternity. They prized it with reverence, they loved it with passion; and because of their devotion to it not a few of them suffered spoiling of their goods, bonds, imprisonments, and exile, and some even death itself. The grave purpose, the intense convictions, of such men lifted them above all puerilities and affectations. It was not for them to seek out artificial refinement or strive to gild refined gold; nor, on the other hand, could they stoop to coarseness or slang. They forgot themselves in their work, and hence the marvellous union it displays, of simplicity and majesty, homeliness and beauty. "They were far more studious of the matter than of the manner; and there is no surer preservative against writing ill or more potent charm for writing well." (Augustus Hare.) Seeking merely to furnish to their fellows the divine oracles in an intelligible form, they not only did that, but gave to all succeeding generations a masterpiece of English composition, one that shows our language at its best, unfolding its varied resources both of vocabulary and of idiom, and offering many striking specimens of its melodious rhythm.

CONSERVATIVE INFLUENCE OF KING JAMES'S VERSION.—No small regard is due to our Bible for its influence in preserving our language from corruption. Time and again there has been an influx of alien elements introduced by a capricious fashion, or by some able but unwise leader. But amid all the vagaries of popular taste, and the changes occasioned by social revolutions, or the progress of knowledge and discovery, this book has stood like a massive breakwater, unyielding and invincible. Perpetually in the hands of the people, used in public and private worship, resorted to in all controversies, employed in schools and education, in short, a daily companion from the cradle to the grave, it has so shaped the tastes and judgments of men that, however for a time misled, they were always in the end recalled to the older and better model, and renewed their adhesion to the pure "well of English undefyled."

OTHER REVISIONS.—That the book deserves what has been claimed for it is shown by its history. When it first came from the press there were two other versions in general use. One of these, the Bishops' Bible, was most prized at court and found in all the churches; the other, the Genevan, was cherished in the household and the closet of the middle classes. Now, no royal edict, no decree of convocation, commanded the use of King James's version, yet simply by its own merits it overpowered both these rivals, and, in the course of a single generation, became the accepted book of the entire nation. In after years repeated attempts were made to introduce a new translation; but they all failed, whether put forth by coxcombs, like the man who improved "Jesus wept" into "Jesus burst into a flood of tears," or by profound and elegant scholars, such as Bishop Lowth, or Dr. George Campbell, of Aberdeen. The reason of the failure was not the perfect correctness of the authorized Scripture: no one claims for it any such infallibility. The progress of Biblical knowledge in very many directions has shown the need of much correction. But the gain of the modern versions, in this respect, was so counterbalanced by the loss in style and tone of feeling that the Christian public would none of them; and these amended Bibles, or parts of Bibles, however loudly heralded, or under whatever high names issued, have passed out of recollection, or are consulted only by curious scholars.

PRESENT REVISION.—The same thing is shown by the principles which underlie the revision now going on in England and America. This is a very elaborate enterprise, undertaken under the highest auspices, and representing, as far as possible, all bodies of English-speaking Christians. In these respects it far exceeds anything of the kind ever attempted before. Yet its conductors announce at the threshold that they neither intend nor desire a new translation; that is not needed, and if accomplished would prove an inevitable failure. All they aim at, therefore, is to make only such corrections as the progress of the language or of Biblical science may render necessary, and in all changes to preserve, as far as possible, the very form and spirit of the existing Bible. Each of them heartily concurs in the judgment pronounced on this point by a late distinguished pervert to Romanism, Dr. F. W. Faber, with whose eloquent and touching words this paper concludes:—

FABER ON KING JAMES'S VERSION.—"Who will say that the uncommon beauty and marvellous English of the Protestant Bible is not one of the great strongholds of heresy in this country? It lives on the ear, like music that can never be forgotten, like the sound of church bells, which the convert hardly knows how he can forego. Its felicities often seem to be almost things rather than words. It is part of the national mind, and the anchor of national seriousness. Nay, it is worshiped with a positive idolatry, in extenuation of whose grotesque fanaticism its intrinsic beauty pleads availingly with the man of letters and the scholar. The memory of the dead passes into it. The potent traditions of childhood are stereotyped in its verses. The power of all the griefs and trials of a man are hid beneath its words. It is the representative of his best moments, and all that there has been about him of soft and gentle, and pure and penitent and good, speaks to him forever out of his Protestant Bible. It is his sacred thing which doubt has never dimmed and controversy never soiled."

REASONS FOR A NEW REVISION OF THE SCRIPTURES IN ENGLISH.

BY THEODORE D. WOOLSEY, D.D., LL.D.,
Ex-President of Yale College.

Valid reasons for a new revision of the Scriptures must be found, if they exist, either in a better acquaintance with the original texts than was possible for those who prepared our authorized English version, or in the advance of scholarship since the beginning of the eighteenth century, or in the changes of the English language within the two centuries and a half since King James's version appeared. Each of these considerations will form, as I understand, the subject of a separate article. It will not be expected, therefore, that the writer should say more on either of them than will be enough to present his case to his readers as a distinct whole, dependent for its justice and force on what others will say more fully and convincingly.

DEMAND FOR REVISIONS.—There is, however, one other consideration, drawn from fact and experience, which deserves to find a place here at the beginning of our remarks. If a translation of a book like the sacred Scriptures were a very easy task, to be undertaken once for all—if the scholarship of the first ages after the conversion of a nation to Christianity could solve all the problems of interpretation which they present—what reason could there be for the repeated demands, in almost every country where Christianity has gained a foothold, for revised and corrected or for wholly new translations? Does not this demand show at once a real want, and a strong desire to reach a better translation than any previous age has produced?

Various Translations.—Let us be permitted to illustrate, by an example or two, the force of this argument, from experience. Origen, the great Christian scholar of the third century after Christ, arranged in parallel columns the Hebrew text of the old Scriptures, both in Hebrew and Greek letters, and seven Greek translations by their side—those of Aquila, Symmachus, the Seventy, Theodotion, and three others, called the fifth, sixth, and seventh editions, of which very little is left on record. In the Syriac there are five or six versions, or recensions, beginning with the Peshito, which goes back to the second century. In our own language, the authorized version of King James makes the ninth translation of the whole or of a considerable part of the Scriptures, not to count quite a number since the Authorized Version appeared, and for which, generally, single persons are responsible.

These illustrations show that as the Christian religion gains firmer hold in a nation, there is a desire felt for a more accurate translation than has been handed down from the past. They seem to show also that there are permanent causes for recensions or revisions of translations, which are acknowledged, like our existing version, to be, on the whole, exceedingly good. What are some of these causes?

1. First Reason for a New Revision.—The first is the gradual change to which languages—at least most languages—are subject. Old words drop out of use, or lose certain meanings, so as to puzzle many readers; or, by being used in new senses, they acquire a certain ambiguity, which needs to be removed, for the sake of the common reader. It is true that a well-executed version, like our English one, tends to preserve a language from

a number of changes which would otherwise be inevitable; but it is true, also, that an ancient translation, preserved on account of the veneration which is felt towards it, may even do harm to religion by obscuring thoughts which would otherwise be clear.

ELEVATION OF BIBLICAL STYLE.—We would here guard against a wrong inference which might be drawn from our remarks, as if in a translation for the nineteenth century, the words most in use in the century, and most familiar to the ears of the people, ought always to take the place of others less in use, which, however, retain their place in the language. This is far from being a safe rule. One of the most important impressions which the Word of God makes is made by its venerableness. The dignity and sanctity of the truth are supported by the elevation of the style, and woe be to the translator who should seek to vulgarize the Bible, on the plea of rendering it more intelligible. Understood it must be, and this must be provided for by removing the ambiguities and obscurities to which changes in society and changes in the expression of thought give rise. But as long as the English is a living tongue, the style of the Scriptures must be majestic, and removed from all vulgarity. Indeed, it must be such as it is now, with those exceptions, few in number, which time brings with it, and most of which will hardly be noticed by the cursory reader.

2. GREEK MANUSCRIPTS.—A second reason for a new revision of our authorized version is found in the scanty knowledge of the state of the original text which was accessible at the time when that version saw the light. The main object in attempting to discover what are the texts followed in manuscripts of the Scriptures, or by

early Christian writers in their citations, or by the early translators into foreign tongues, is to ascertain, as far as possible, just what was written or dictated by the sacred writers. The scribes and other authorities to whom we owe our texts were subject to the same mistakes with any other copyists; and it is of the first importance that we should know what text, in any given case, is to be preferred to other readings. For the performance of this most laborious task there were, in the early part of the seventeenth century, no adequate materials accessible. The great accumulation of readings, and the new conviction of the importance of the critical art, in its application to the sacred text, began about the eighteenth century. Since then, above all, in the later times, multitudes of scholars have devoted themselves to the collation of manuscripts and of early versions. Numbers of manuscripts, and among them some of the most ancient, have been discovered, and the citations in the Fathers have been examined with care. The ages of manuscripts also, and the rules for estimating their comparative value, are fixed with greater precision. The skill of textual critics, and the means within their reach for determining the texts are such as to assure us, in most cases, what was the original reading; and this important end has been reached by the zeal and labors of men who have lived long since 1611, when the first edition of our present English Bible was printed.

It may frighten some of our readers to be told that there are many thousand different readings in the New Testament, collected by the labors of scholars; but they ought to be assured that the text is more certain by far than if there had been only as many hundreds, and the mass of authorities for the text had been unconsulted.

3. Defects in King-James's Version.—The third reason for a new revision, and the last which I shall mention, is that our translators of the seventeenth century, in a great many instances, misunderstood the sense. To make this as evident as it may be made we should need to write a volume. Such volumes have been written; among which Dr. Lightfoot's work on "A Fresh Revision of the English New Testament" may be commended as the best. In this brief paper we can only say that the main deficiency in our translation proceeds from want of exact knowledge of the Hebrew and Greek languages. Not only is the sense wholly misapprehended in a number of instances—as could scarcely fail of being the case—but a perception of the finer rules of grammar and interpretation was wanting. In the use of the article, of the tenses and modes of verbs, and of participles, and in a great variety of other instances, the modern scholar by his revisions can repair and beautify the building reared by the older scholars. Thus, while no book can be written more fitted in style and expression to do its work, more truly English, more harmonious, more simply majestic, than our authorized revision; new revisers of the text and the version may hope—by their salutary changes—to contribute to its preservation, in essentially the same form which it has always had, for generations yet to come.

THE CURRENT VERSION OF THE SCRIPTURES, AS COMPARED WITH OUR PRESENT NEEDS.

BY G. EMLEN HARE, D.D., L.L.D.,

Professor of Biblical Learning in the Divinity School of the Protestant Episcopal Church, Philadelphia.

The current version of the Scriptures is commonly known as the "Authorized." The epithet may have originated in the fact that the book bears on its title page the words "Appointed to be read in churches." But that the appointment thus mentioned—that of the monarch reigning in England at the time of the publication—was not the source of the authority of the version, is manifest from the fact that the book did not come into general use in English churches for something like half a century after the time the appointment was made. The authority of the work came from its superiority to the translations previously in use and the general recognition which this superiority deserved and obtained.

Two hundred and sixty-eight years have intervened between the publication of the English Bible and the present time. During this interval multitudes of words have changed their meaning. The phrases "by," "by and by," and "charger," may serve as examples. St. Paul says, in the Authorized Version (1 Cor. iv, 4), "I know nothing by myself, yet am I not hereby justified." This seems incongruous, because "to know nothing by one's self" means "to know nothing originally or independently." In the older English, "to know nothing by one's self" meant "to know nothing lying at one's door," and this is the only sense of which the Greek words in the passage which seems so incongruous are susceptible. He who reads the Gospel of St. Mark in Greek gets a vivid idea of the promptitude, the tendency to strike while the iron is hot, which cunning and malice may engender. A princess enters the banqueting room of a king, enchants him by the grace of her dancing, and evokes from his tipsy rashness the promise, "Ask what thou wilt and I will give it thee, even to the half of my kingdom." (St. Mark vi, 22.) The damsel, after consulting with her mother, returns to the banqueting room, points, no doubt, to the dishes on the banqueting table, and says, "Give me forthwith, on a dish, the head of John the Baptist." In the English Bible the speech runs, "Give me by and by, in a charger." "By and by" means, in our century, a time somewhat distant from the present; the phrase has ceased to mean "forthwith." A charger, in modern English, signifies a war horse; the word has ceased to signify a dish or platter from which plates are charged or supplied. If the Bible is intended for the less educated of the Christian Church it needs, in many places, to be translated out of the older into the later English.

Within the two hundred and sixty-eight years which have elapsed since the publication of the Current Version Biblical learning has advanced with a progress comparable to that which has obtained in other departments of learning. Ten times as many manuscripts of the New Testament as were known to our venerable translators have been discovered since their time, and that kind of criticism which judges of the age of ancient manuscripts and determines the true reading where copies differ, has been reduced to a science. In many places textual criticism is unanimous, at the present day, in favor of readings more or less different from those which the authors of the present version followed. "Alexander, the coppersmith, did me much evil: the Lord reward him according to his works." (2 Tim. iv, 14.) The true reading yields the sense, "Alexander, the coppersmith, did me much evil; the Lord will reward him according to his works."

St. Paul, speaking of Abraham, says, "He considered not his own body now dead, . . . neither yet the deadness of Sarah's womb: he staggered not at the promise of God through unbelief." (Rom. iv, 19.) This statement conflicts with the history in the book of Genesis. This history is so far from representing Abraham as *not* considering at the time mentioned, that it declares that Abraham said in his heart, "Shall *a child* be born unto him that is a hundred years old? and shall Sarah, that is ninety years old, bear?" (Gen. xvii, 17.) Textual critics agree in reading the language of St. Paul without the word "not." They so determine the text as to translate "He considered his own body now dead and the deadness of Sarah's womb, but staggered not at the promise of God through unbelief." Such decisions of critics are made in accordance with rules which recognize the more difficult of two readings as being, *cæteris paribus*, the more worthy of acceptance. Ought not English readers to have the benefit of their knowledge?

Our translators say, in their noble preface, that they have not been studious of an "identity of phrasing;" that is to say, they acknowledge that they have not been careful to render a Hebrew or Greek word by the same English phrase in the different places where the Hebrew or Greek word occurs. Yet an identity of phrasing is often necessary as a clue to the meaning.

Moses saw an Egyptian smiting a Hebrew and he slew the Egyptian, says the English Bible. (Ex. ii, 11, 12.) In this sentence the same Hebrew word is translated in the first instance by the word "smiting," and in the second instance by the word "slew." If the Hebrew word had been translated "slaying" in the place where it is translated "smiting" the meaning would have been more perceptible and the act of Moses less liable to misconstruction. In the earlier books of the Old Testament a remarkable person appears under the name of the "Angel of the Lord." For example, when the covenant with Abraham was to be ratified the language of Genesis is, "The Angel of the Lord called unto Abraham, . . . in blessing I will bless thee, and in multiplying I will multiply thy seed . . . . thy seed shall possess the gate of his enemies; and in thy seed shall all the nations of the earth be blessed." (Gen. xxii, 15, 17, 18.) Here the Angel of the Lord appears as covenanting. In Exodus the same person under the same name appears as covenanted, "I send an Angel before thee, . . . beware of him, . . . for my name *is* in him." There is a remarkable passage in the book of Malachi (iii, 1), which, if translated with the identity of phrasing that our translators disregarded, would run, "the Lord whom ye seek shall suddenly come to his temple, even the Angel of the Covenant, whom ye delight in." Unhappily, in this passage of Malachi the word "messenger" is used where the Hebrew word is the same as that which is rendered "Angel" in the places of Genesis and Exodus. He who reads the Old Testament in the original may come to the conclusion that *the* Angel of *the* Covenant, promised by Malachi, was to be the same being as had appeared in the Pentateuch, one while as covenanting, another while as covenanted. The common reader ought to have the benefit of an identity of phrasing where this identity is necessary in order to identify the thing or person meant.

The priest's lips should keep knowledge, that the people may seek the law at his mouth. In 1870 priests awoke to this truth. The Convocation of Canterbury, the oldest synod in English speaking Christendom, appointed a Committee to revise the current version of the Scriptures. This Committee was to make no change for the sake of change. It was not to desert the style of the English Bible. It was to invite the coöperation of Biblical scholars of different nations and creeds, and was to give ten years to the important project. Eight of these ten years have elapsed. Scholars of this country, as well as scholars of Great Britain, are engaged in the work. What will be the issue? The Latin version of the Scriptures, made by Jerome, was for a thousand years the standard Bible of Western Christendom. Yet the making of it was earnestly opposed, and the work did not establish itself in general acceptance for two centuries. May the Revision at present in progress meet with earlier success: may Christian people give the work the benefit of their prayers, and when it appears give the book a candid reception!

THE HEBREW TEXT OF THE OLD TESTAMENT.

BY HOWARD OSGOOD, D.D.,

Professor of Hebrew, in Rochester Theological Seminary.

THE HISTORY OF THE TEXT.—The Hebrew text, as we now find it in the best editions of the Old Testament, is a reprint, with few and slight exceptions, of the text edited by Jewish scholars, and printed by Bomberg, at Venice, in 1525, and reprinted by him, with corrections, in 1547. In some of the subsequent editions of the text, a few manuscripts and the preceding printed editions were compared, and errors corrected; but until the latter part of the last century there was no text published which was founded upon a large comparison of manuscripts.

Bomberg's Hebrew text was accompanied by Rabbinic commentaries, and was designed for the use of the Jews, since few Christians at that day understood Hebrew, and still fewer were acquainted with Rabbinic. This text enjoys the great advantage of being acknowledged as the received text by Jews and Christians alike. That it is worthy of great confidence is the united testimony of critics, and one of the latest and most learned, Strack, makes stronger statements in favor of the preservation of the correct reading in this text than some of his predecessors, or than is welcome to some who cannot but admire his preëminent ability and learning.

We do not know what or how many manuscripts were used by the editors of this text, but from the preface to the Bible of 1525, and from the carefulness in editing, we are assured that the principal editor, Jacob ben Chayim, was as thoroughly skilled in the text as in the then known various readings; and that he was as reverent to the text as he was learned. Whatever manuscripts were used, they were in all probability of a late date, written under the strict and microscopic rules of the Talmud, and accompanied with the various readings of the Masorites. In respect to age, no extant Hebrew manuscript can compare with the Sinaitic and Vatican Greek manuscripts; and yet, in verification of the text, the Hebrew possesses a line of witnesses that extends a long way down the centuries, and who have sought to guard the text with scrupulous care.

When the privileges of the great Jewish schools in Babylonia were restricted by the Persian kings, and the greater part of the Talmud had been collected, the intense activity of the Jewish brain, and Jewish devotion to the very letter of the word, were directed to the notation of all diversities in the traditional reading of the text, as to consonants, vowels, accents, words, the commencement and close of verses and divisions of the text, as well as to any unusual marks found in manuscripts. They marked with all care mistakes in any of these points, but never altered the text. Even where the mistake was evident and trivial—a letter slightly out of place, or upside down, or too small, or too large, or a variation in the writing of a word—they did not presume to change the text. This honest dealing with the text is represented in our Bibles to-day by the continuance of the mistake and its attendant corrective margin. These textual criticisms were originally contained in separate works, but were afterwards transferred to the margin of the manuscripts of the Hebrew Old Testament, and by the labors of scholars of our day they are again being collected and published in separate works.

In the era of the Talmudists, before A.D. 500, very strict rules were enjoined upon copyists. These rules cover all the minutiæ of composition, and reveal a method of dealing with the text that must have been traditional. The attention the Talmudists themselves bestowed upon the text is shown by their enumeration of the verses, words and letters of each book, and their designation of the middle verse, word and letter of the book.

Within this same period Jerome, in his translation, corrects renderings of the Septuagint, and gives us a faithful representation of the text then received in Palestine. No large additions or defections from that text are found in our own.

The boast of Josephus, that "during so many ages as have already passed no one has been so bold as either to add anything to them" (the sacred books), "to take anything from them, or to make any change in them," seems to be justified by the minute traditional rules and carefulness of the later Jews.

All this shows us that for fifteen centuries, at least, it was a religious duty with the Jews to preserve, with all exactness, the sacred text as received by them: a duty which they zealously sought to perform. When the Hebrew language was unknown by Christians, when the Jew was under the harrow of unresting persecution and his name a byword, he was with patient fidelity keeping watch over the text, unknown to all but himself, and preserving a priceless inheritance for the coming centuries. As respects the Hebrew text, "Japheth dwells in the tents of Shem."

The Accuracy of the Present Text.—That there are passages where the text has suffered from wrong transcription, where there are insuperable difficulties or slight mistakes, where manuscripts differ, and versions give a rendering at variance with the present text, is well known to every Hebrew scholar. If with the superior advantages of the printing press for the maintenance of a given text, with our Bible societies and multitudes of critical readers of the English Bible, we have not preserved one and the same text in all the editions, is it a matter of astonishment that manuscripts vary? Is it not a matter of greater astonishment if they agree in most respects, written, as they were, centuries apart? But these places where error has crept in are by no means so numerous as some critics would have us believe. Dr. S. Davidson, a very competent critic, in his "Revision of the Hebrew Text," cites between seven and eight thousand places where manuscripts and versions differ from our text. These changes, for the far greater part, refer to the different modes of writing or accentuating the same word; they include the thousand or more marginal notes of the Jewish mediæval scholars, the changes of the vowel by the accent, etc.

The Old Testament contains more than three times as much text as the New Testament, and if we put the diversities of readings in the Old Testament at ten thousand, still this would be but one-fifteenth as many as those found in the manuscripts of the New Testament. As the one hundred and fifty thousand various readings of the New Testament dwindle to a comparatively very small number when you apply the touchstone of a change of signification, so the Old Testament ten thousand dwindle at the same test. It should be remembered that if for the criticism of the Old Testament we possessed a critical apparatus as full as that for the New the number of diversities might be largely increased.

That the true text may be established in every part, and portion of the Word must be the aim of every earnest student. The means for establishing the text are the collation of all known manuscripts; the wise use of the results of Jewish criticism of the text in the earlier centuries; the early versions, and the printed editions.

The utmost diligence in the search for ancient Hebrew manuscripts has failed to bring to light any manuscript of which we can be certain that its age is greater than a thousand years, though some have been discovered for which a higher antiquity is claimed. The Herculean labors of Kennicott and of De Rossi in the last century have not resulted in establishing beyond controversy, among critics, any material change in the text. They have added but little to what was known before. In this century Frankel, Frensdorf, Pinsker, Strack, and others have brought out a greater number of the diversities marked by the early Jewish scholars, and the forthcoming work of Ginsburg promises to be a long step in advance in this direction.

It is proposed by some critics to use the Talmud, the so-called Chaldee translations, and the Septuagint, to restore the Hebrew in places where they differ from it. But to restore the text in doubtful places we must have exact knowledge and abundant proof. Some great scholars have tried their hand at restoration, and now serve the excellent purpose of warnings. Capellus, Houbigant, Kennicott, Lowth, and some in this century, have wasted their strength in mending the text to suit their views, and their work is rejected by their critics. That which seems perfectly feasible proves, in the doing of it, to be exceedingly difficult. To attempt to restore the Hebrew text by a means that we are not entirely sure of is certainly not wise. Neither the Talmud, nor any one of the Chaldee translations, nor the Septuagint, has been submitted to a thorough critical revision. One of the crying needs of Old Testament study is a trustworthy edition of the Septuagint, and until that is obtained the Septuagint cannot safely be used, as of itself a strong argument for the change of text.

Though scholars have not now at their command the means to enter upon a thorough critical revision of the Hebrew text, yet it is probable that the work will not be long delayed, for never before were there so many earnest and well qualified students engaged upon this subject, and we may look forward with hope and confidence to their results: with hope that light will be thrown upon difficult passages; with confidence that no great changes will be found necessary.

The Duty of a Translator.—The labors of past centuries have proved that our present text, as a whole, is worthy of all confidence. The translator is not to suppose an error where he finds a difficulty. The error must be unmistakably proved before he concedes it. We have numerous instances of the assumption of error in the text because the student meets with a difficulty that seems to him insuperable. There is a striking example of this in a writer on the orthodox side asserting an interpolation and utter error in Deuteronomy, while a critic, who professes himself by no means orthodox, argues stoutly against the supposition of error in the text, and has all the critical evidence on his side.

Nor is the translator to make his text. There are some who are capable of the double work of accurate textual criticism and translating the text obtained, but they are very few. The translator is to keep with all faithfulness to the text the best scholarship brings to him, and he will find all his energies tasked to the utmost to represent that most exactly and acceptably in his own tongue. Where there can be no doubt of an error in the text, then the text and margin of the translation must tell the story.

HEBREW PHILOLOGY AND BIBLICAL SCIENCE.

SHALL THE AUTHORIZED VERSION KEEP PACE WITH THE ADVANCES MADE IN HEBREW PHILOLOGY AND BIBLICAL SCIENCE?

BY THE REV. W. HENRY GREEN, D.D.,

Professor of Oriental and Old Testament Literature in the Theological Seminary at Princeton, N. J.

ADVANCES IN PHILOLOGY AND BIBLICAL SCIENCE.—Moses strictly charged the people, " Ye shall not add unto the word which I command you, neither shall ye diminish aught from it " (Deut. iv, 2; xii, 32). And almost the last utterance of Holy Scripture—Rev. xxii, 18, 19—is a like solemn admonition, neither to add unto, nor to take away from, the words which God had revealed. If, then, it is the imperative duty of the Church to give the heavenly oracles to men, each in his own language, it is equally her duty to give them to men in a pure and unadulterated form. The millions in both hemispheres who speak the English tongue are entitled to receive the Bible in a form which represents the inspired original with the utmost accuracy that it is possible to attain. This has always been recognized in the history of our English version thus far, which, as at present authorized, is the result of several successive revisions, each being an advance upon its predecessor. When the question is raised whether the time has now arrived for a fresh revision of the English Bible, one important consideration affecting the answer to be given is to be found in the immense strides taken in Biblical scholarship since the reign of King James. The object of this brief paper is to indicate this in a few particulars relating to the Old Testament.

HEBREW PHILOLOGY IN 1611.—Hebrew studies were then in their infancy, and the entire science of Semitic philology has been developed since. When the first edition of the Authorized Version appeared, in 1611, the elder Buxtorf had just issued his larger Hebrew grammar, in 1609, his smaller grammar having been published in 1605, and his Hebrew lexicon in 1607. Buxtorf's Hebrew Concordance first saw the light in 1632. The two Buxtorfs, father and son, though men of immense learning and indefatigable industry, represent the first stage of investigation into the structure and meaning of the Hebrew language. They brought together all that could be gathered from Rabbinical lore and from traditional interpretations. But there their work ended. Since their time the knowledge of Hebrew has been greatly increased by the comparative study of the kindred dialects, the Syriac, Arabic and Ethiopic; the meanings of many of its words have been more satisfactorily established, and its various constructions have been elucidated. A long list of able lexicographers, from Castellus to Gesenius and Fuerst, and of distinguished grammarians, from Schultens to Ewald, have been pushing their researches more and more thoroughly into this venerable and sacred tongue. And commentators without end, approaching the subject from every different point of view, and of widely dissimilar opinions, have minutely discussed every word and sentence of the sacred text, and labored with various success to bring out the fullness of its meaning. The great polyglotts, particularly that of Paris in 1645, and that of London in 1657, set the old Syriac and Arabic versions alongside of the Hebrew text, with a view to ready comparison and aid to interpretation, as Buxtorf's Rabbinical Bible, in 1618, had done with the Chaldee targums and the comments of the Rabbins.

MASORETIC TEXT.—The extensive and laborious collections of Hebrew manuscripts by Houbigant, Kennicott, and De Rossi have done little more than establish the substantial correctness of the received Masoretic text. And the long and earnest discussion relative to the Hebrew vowels has resulted in proving, if not their originality, at least their accuracy. We stand upon precisely the same text, therefore, as King James's translators used, only with a better knowledge of its value.

NEED OF IMPROVEMENT IN THE VERSION OF 1611.—But the helps to a better understanding of this text have accumulated immensely. Besides the philological aids already referred to, there is the increased knowledge of sacred localities, and of the natural history and archæology of the Bible, derived from travels and explorations in the Holy Land, and from the monuments exhumed in Assyria, Egypt and elsewhere. This, of course, assists us in the comprehension of passages in which such objects are referred to, and consequently enables us to translate them with greater accuracy and precision.

GEOGRAPHICAL ERRORS.—It would be clearly impossible, in a popular article of a few columns, to give an accurate conception of what has been accomplished, in these various lines of scholarship, toward the elucidation of the Old Testament, and of the extent to which this renders it possible now to improve a translation made more than two hundred and fifty years ago. Only a few illustrations can now be attempted, taken very much at random. Thus, many geographical terms require correction. For example, "the river of Egypt," Numbers xxxiv, 5, and elsewhere, would naturally lead one to think of the Nile; it is not this, however, which is intended, but an insignificant stream that bounds Egypt on the east, "the brook of Egypt." The "Palestina" of Isaiah xiv, 29–31, and the "Palestine" of Joel iii, 4, is simply "Philistia," the territory occupied by the Philistines. The second river of the garden of Eden did not compass the "land of Ethiopia," but that of "Cush," settled by a people so called from their progenitor. Ezekiel xxix, 10; xxx, 6, does not speak of desolating Egypt "from the tower of Syene even unto the border of Ethiopia," for Syene was itself on that border, but "from Migdol unto Syene," *i.e.*, from the extreme north to the extreme south of Egypt, "even unto the border of Ethiopia." The "mount Ephraim" of Josh. xxiv, 33, and elsewhere, is not a single summit, but an elevated tract, "the hill country of Ephraim." "The valley" of Josh. xi, 16, should be "the lowland;" "the south," Gen. xii, 9, and elsewhere, is not simply the general designation of a point of the compass, but the name of a definite tract of country, and as such should begin with a capital letter—"the South." The "rough valley" of Deut. xxi, 4, should be "a valley with an overflowing stream." The "nation scattered and peeled," "whose land the rivers have spoiled," Isa. xviii, 2, should be the "nation tall and shaven," "whose land the rivers divide." Samuel's father was not "an Ephrathite," 1 Sam. i, 1, as though he were from Ephrata or Bethlehem, but "an Ephraimite," so reckoned because he resided in the territory of Ephraim, though descended from Levi.

ERRORS IN PROPER NAMES.—Proper names have sometimes been mistaken for common nouns or other parts of speech, and translated accordingly; and, conversely, words which should have been translated are retained as though they were proper names. Thus, "the house of God," Judges xx, 26, should be "Bethel;" "an hollow place that was in the jaw," Judges xv, 19, should be "the hollow place that is in Lehi;" "populous No," Nah. iii, 8, should be "No-Ammon;" "an heifer of three years old," Isa. xv, 5, should have been left untranslated; so should "what he did," Num. xxi, 14. On the contrary, "the book of Jasher," 2 Sam. i, 18, is not by an author of that name, but is simply the book of the upright. "Rab-saris" and "Rab-mag," Jer. xxxix, 3, are not names of men, but titles of office. "Belial" is not the name of an evil spirit, but "men of Belial" ought to be rendered "worthless" or "base men." "Huzzab," Nah. ii, 7, is not a personification of Nineveh, or a name of its queen, but a declaration that the fate of the city "is decided." "Sheth," Num. xxiv, 17, should be "tumult;" "Bajith," Isa. xv, 2, should be the "house" or "idol temple;" "Gammadims," Ezek. xxvii, 11, should be "warriors;" "Pannag," ver. 17, is not a region of country, but a species of confection; and there was no such place as "Metheg-ammah," 2 Sam. viii, 1.

MISTAKES OF THE MEANING.—A few instances occur in which words of a peculiar formation have been entirely mistaken by our translators, and divided into two words when they are in reality one. Thus, the word translated "thick clay," Hab. ii, 6, is not a compound term yielding this sense, but a reduplicated form from a single root, and means "pledges," or goods taken in pledge by an extortionate creditor; and "shameful spewing," ver. 16, is but a single word meaning "ignominy." The awkward expression, Hos. iv, 18, "her rulers with shame do love, Give ye," should be rendered, "her rulers are in love with shame." The "scape goat" of Lev. xvi, 8, is one word, not two, and has no reference to the goat at all.

The cases are frequent in which the meanings of words are altogether mistaken, although the forms are not misconceived nor the words improperly divided. Thus, the word translated "avenging," Judges v, 2, means "leaders;" "the plain of Moreh," Gen. xii, 6, ought to be "the oak of Moreh;" "the groves," so frequently spoken of in connection with idolatrous services, as Ex. xxxiv, 13, were not groves, but upright pillars. Job. xxvi, 13, does not speak of the "crooked," nor Isaiah xxvii, 1, of the "piercing" serpent; the epithet, which is the same in both cases, is "fleet." The psalmist does not say, Ps. lxxi, 22, "I will sing with the harp," but "I will play with the harp." Huldah did not dwell in the "college," 2 Kings xxii, 14, but in the "second ward" of the city. "Since that time," Isa. xvi, 13, should be "of old;" "flagons of wine," Hos. iii, 1, should be "cakes of pressed grapes;" "galleries," Cant. vii, 5, should be "curls" or "locks of hair." Hosea xi, 12, does not use the language of praise, "Judah yet ruleth with God," but of censure, "he roveth or runs wild in his dealings with him." Isaiah ix, 1, does not contrast a former light affliction of Galilee with a subsequent more grievous affliction of the same region, but the period of dishonor with the glory that was to be shed upon that region by the coming Redeemer. "All that make sluices and ponds for fish," Isa. xix, 10, is a mere guess from the connection, and should be rendered, "all that work for hire are sad at heart." Samson did not go down to "the top of the rock," Judges xv, 8, but to the "cleft of the rock." The children of Israel did not by divine direction "borrow," Ex. xi, 2, of the Egyptians what they never intended to return; they "asked" for and received gifts. "Chariots with flaming torches," Nah. ii, 3, are "chariots with flashing steel;" and "the fir trees" of the same verse are lances made of cypress. "Hunt souls to make them fly," Ezek. xiii, 20, should be rendered, "hunt souls as birds;" and the "untempered mortar," ver. 10, should be "whitewash."

Such mistakes are especially frequent in articles of dress or in objects of natural history. The "headbands, and tablets, and earrings," Isa. iii, 20, should be "sashes, and perfume boxes, and amulets." Joseph's "coat of many colors," Gen. xxxvii, 3, was instead "a long tunic with sleeves." It was not a "veil" but a "mantle," Ruth iii, 15, in which Ruth carried the barley. "Pillows to all armholes," Ezek. xiii, 18, should be "cushions for the knuckles." The men that were cast into the fiery furnace were bound, not in "their coats, their hosen and their hats," but in "their trowsers, their tunics, and their mantles." The Chaldeans, Ezek. xxiii, 15, "exceeding with dyed attire," wore "flowing turbans," and the best illustration of the entire description is to be found in the figures portrayed on the palaces of Nineveh. The "mules,"

Gen. xxxvi, 24, ought to be rendered, "warm springs." The "unicorn," Num. xxiii, 22, is a wild ox. In Isaiah xiii, 21, 22, the "owls" are "ostriches;" the "satyrs" are "goats;" the "wild beasts of the islands" are "wolves," and the "dragons" are "jackals."

ERRORS IN HEBREW GRAMMAR.—There are, besides, many passages in which the rendering given in the Authorized Version is in violation of the laws of Hebrew grammar. The most frequently recurring error is the disregard of the tenses, particularly in the poetical and prophetical books of the Old Testament, to the serious detriment, and often to the total obscuration of the sense. In Ps. iii, 4, David does not say, "I cried" and "he heard," and ver. 5, "the Lord sustained," as though he were relating what had already taken place; but "I will cry," "he will hear," "the Lord will sustain:" it is the language of confident expectation. Ps. xxxvii, 40, should not be translated, "the Lord shall help them and deliver them," but he "has helped them and delivered them;" it is a fact of former experience, from which he then goes on to infer that he will do the same in the future, "he shall deliver them from the wicked and save them." By the neglect of the tenses the two clauses are made identical in sense, and the whole argument of faith is lost. In Ps. xl, 11, David does not say, "Withhold not thou thy tender mercies," but "thou wilt not withhold;" it is not the language of petition, but of faith. In Obadiah, vs. 12–14, the verbs should be rendered, "look not," "rejoice not," etc., instead of "thou shouldest not have looked," "thou shouldest not have rejoiced," etc. Hab. iii, 3, should not be "God came," but "God will come." The language of the Authorized

Version implies that these prophets were narrating or referring to what was past; whereas they are predicting the future.

This confusing of the tenses is of almost perpetual occurrence in the Psalms and in the Prophets, leading to serious inversions in the order of thought, and marring the beauty and force of the language used.

Disregard of the Definite Article.—Another frequent inaccuracy is the disregard of the definite article, either failing to render it where it does occur, or inserting it where it is not. Sometimes this is attended with serious detriment to the sense, as where "an angel of the Lord" is substituted for "the angel of the Lord," a created for the uncreated angel. Judges xxi, 19, should not read, "There is a feast of the Lord in Shiloh," but "the feast of the Lord is in Shiloh;" it is spoken of not with vague indefiniteness, but as a definite, well-known observance.

Inaccuracy in the Construction.—It may be added that there is frequently an inaccuracy in the construction, as where possessive pronouns are attached to the wrong noun. Thus, Ps. iv, 1, David addresses the Lord not as the Authorized Version has it, "God of my righteousness," as though his meaning were the God who defends my righteous cause, but "my righteous God." Ps. lix, 17, not "God of my mercy," but "my merciful God." Ps. xlvii, 8, not "the throne of his holiness;" Ps. xlviii, 1, not "the mountain of his holiness," but "his holy throne," "his holy mountain." Isa. xiii, 3, not "them that rejoice in my highness," but "my proud exulters." Errors in relative constructions, *e.g.*, Isa. vii, 16, not "the land, that thou abhorrest, shall be forsaken of both her kings," but "the land, of whose two kings thou art afraid, shall be forsaken." Ps. lv, 19, not "God shall hear and afflict them. Because they have no changes, therefore they fear not God," but "God shall hear and answer them, who have no changes and who fear not God," *i.e.*, as he heard me in mercy, ver. 17, so he will hear them in wrath, answering not their prayers, for they do not pray, but the voice of their malignant slanders. And other miscellaneous constructions, which it is needless to particularize in further detail, *e.g.*, Ezek. xxxiv, 31, not "ye my flock are men," but "ye men are my flock." Ps. vii, 13, not "ordaineth his arrows against the persecutors," but "maketh his arrows burning." Ps. x, 4, not "God is not in all his thoughts," but "all his thoughts are, There is no God." Ps. xix, 3, not "There is no speech nor language *where* their voice is not heard," as though the Psalmist were speaking of the universality of God's self-revelation in nature. The insertion of the italic word "*where*" entirely deranges the relation of the clauses, and introduces a totally different thought from that which David intended. He means that all nature has a voice, though it is not addressed to man's outward ear. "There is no speech nor language; their voice is not heard." Ps. xxii, 30, not "it shall be accounted unto the Lord for a generation," but "it shall be related of the Lord unto the next generation." Num. xxiii, 23, not "Surely there is no enchantment against Jacob, neither is there any divination against Israel: according to the time it shall be said of Jacob and of Israel, What hath God wrought!" The meaning is not that God's divine power will effectually guard Israel against all hostile arts of enchantment: but Israel has no need to resort to deceptive and unauthorized modes of learning the divine will, for this will is disclosed to them as their needs may require. "There is no enchantment in Jacob, nor divination in Israel; at the time it shall be told to Jacob and Israel what God hath wrought." The italic words, *into a trance,* Num. xxiv, 4, obscure the statement of the overpowering physical effect produced upon Balaam by the splendor of the divine revelations. The italic words, *to wit,* improperly inserted in Josh. xvii, 1, precisely reverse the meaning of the clause. It is designed to explain why no lot was cast for Machir now; the reason is, because his possession had already been assigned to him east of the Jordan.

Duty of Revisionists.—Such illustrations could be multiplied. Those which have been already given are sufficient to show that, with the light that has been shed upon the Hebrew language, and the increased information gained upon subjects collateral to the study of the Old Testament since the days of King James, a great number of passages are understood now in a sense different from that given by our translators. To make those corrections in the renderings which the general voice of the best scholars affirms ought to be made, is not to unsettle the Scriptures and to weaken their hold upon the public mind, but the reverse. Innovations are not to be recklessly or needlessly made. But the removal of palpable errors and mistakes is simply extracting the fly from the pot of ointment. The marvel is not that occasional changes are needed to increase the perfection of the Authorized Version and to bring it nearer to the standard of the best biblical scholarship of the time, but that, considering the period when it was made and the scanty helps which were then possessed, the changes required are not more numerous and more radical. It is absolutely astonishing to find to how large an extent this grand old version must be confessed to be still the most adequate and accurate translation that can now be made; and how vast a proportion of its renderings can be subjected to the most rigorous tests that modern learning can apply without the detection of a single flaw.

THE HELPS FOR TRANSLATING THE HEBREW SCRIPTURES AT THE TIME THE AUTHORIZED VERSION WAS MADE.

BY REV. GEORGE E. DAY, D.D.,
Professor of Hebrew Literature and Biblical Theology in Yale College.

Of the forty-eight scholars to whom we owe the present Authorized Version of the English Bible, twenty-five, divided into three companies, were engaged upon the Hebrew books of the Old Testament. There is no reason to doubt their qualifications for the work. Several of them were eminent in oriental studies. One had the reputation of being the best Arabic scholar of his time. Five of them, either then, or subsequently, were professors of Hebrew in one or the other of the two great Universities of England. Their renderings show that they carefully weighed the considerations on which the translation of difficult passages must depend, and exercised an independent judgment. To a great degree they came to what the critical scholarship of later times has pronounced a correct decision. In other cases, where they were divided in opinion, or admitted that a different rendering from that which they adopted was worthy of consideration, they placed it, in a true Protestant spirit, in the margin. If these marginal readings and other renderings, in consequence of the progress of exegetical study, have been frequently found to deserve the preference, it only shows that the scholars of the early part of the seventeenth century were not provided, and could not be, with all the helps for a decision which have accumulated since their day. The division of labor in the whole field of the Hebrew and its cognate languages enables a student, in our time, to avail himself of advantages for gaining a true knowledge of the meaning of the Old Testament which the most stupendous learning of a former age knew nothing of. Nothing, of course, can ever take the place of a familiar acquaintance with the Hebrew and other Semitic languages; but it is quite possible for an interpreter now, in consequence of the far wider range of materials at his command, to form a judgment on a difficult passage more trustworthy than it was possible for the most eminent scholars two centuries and a half ago to reach.

The force of this remark will best be seen from a rapid survey of the learned helps for the interpretation of the Old Testament accessible to the translators of the Authorized Version.

Less than a century had passed since the Lutheran Reformation, and though the impulse given to Hebrew studies in the Christian Church had been immense, and many of the principal sources of knowledge, in respect to the Hebrew Bible, were within their reach, yet the apparatus of scholarship at their command would be regarded in our day as quite imperfect. The text, indeed, had received the fixed form adopted by the Jewish scholars who gave to it its present punctuation. No manuscripts of an earlier date exist with which we can compare it, and the chief superiority, therefore, of the modern printed editions arises from the more careful editing of the Masoretic text, with the apparatus of vowels and accents, and the addition of selected critical notes, which have been transmitted to us from an early period.

But when we come to the *ancient translations*, on which so much depends for the verification of the

Hebrew text and the proper rendering of the Hebrew Scriptures, the case is widely different. The earliest of these, in Greek,—the Septuagint, so called — made, in part at least, in the third century before Christ and in common use in the early Christian Church, was accessible to King James's translators in the Complutensian and Antwerp Polyglots, and also in separate editions; but the Alexandrian manuscript in the British Museum and the Sinaitic manuscript discovered by Tischendorf, as well as the critical labors expended upon the several copies of this venerable Greek version by eminent scholars in England and on the Continent, have furnished the materials for a much more accurate text than any which was possible when the Authorized Version was made. Since then, also, the fragments preserved in the works of Origen, of the translations into Greek by Aquila, Theodotion, Symmachus, and others, made after the Christian era, have been placed at the service of scholars.

The Latin Vulgate, another most important ancient version, was of course in their hands. On many passages their decision was determined by its renderings, on the ground, which cannot be questioned, that the testimony of a learned scholar like Jerome, with the opportunities he enjoyed for becoming acquainted with the accepted Jewish interpretation of his day, is deserving of special consideration. Yet this version has suffered so many changes and corruptions, in the course of ages, that it cannot be relied upon, in its present form, as giving in all cases the exact renderings of Jerome. The book of Psalms, as it stands in the Vulgate, is an earlier version made by him. Whoever wishes to learn his final judgment, must consult the more correct translation which he afterwards made.

It is only within a few years that the Codex Amiatinus, which contains Jerome's own translation of the Old Testament, in distinction from the text found in the ordinary editions of the Vulgate, has been made accessible to scholars.

With the early Syriac translation of the Old Testament, the third most important ancient version, the translators of our Authorized Version could have had no acquaintance. Its value lies in its correctness, and its being in a language cognate to Hebrew, and consequently affording special means of comparison. It was first printed in the Paris Polyglot more than thirty years after the Authorized Version appeared, and was followed at a later period by the publication of another Syriac translation, which, however, is of less value because made from the Septuagint.

Without going further into details, we may say in general that the only ancient versions of the Old Testament accessible to scholars at the beginning of the seventeenth century, except a few single books or parts, were imperfect texts of the Septuagint, the Targums or Chaldee paraphrases, and the Vulgate. The other ancient translations, the Samaritan version of the Pentateuch, the Syriac and Arabic versions, and parts of the Ethiopic and Persian versions contained in the later Polyglots, were not published until many years after the English translation of 1611, and could have made no contribution either directly or indirectly, towards determining its renderings.

The philological helps accessible to the scholars who made our Authorized Version would now be considered quite rudimentary. The larger Hebrew Grammar of the elder Buxtorf appeared shortly before their work was finished (1609). It was in advance certainly of the rude attempts of the few grammarians before his time, whether Rabbinic or Christian, but in contrast with the elaborate and exhaustive grammars of Ewald and Böttcher, or the more compendious treatises of Gesenius and Green, it is exceedingly meagre. The latest and best lexicon at their command was Buxtorf's, which appeared in 1067, just as they were commencing their labors. The help to be gained from the Rabbins and the Vulgate he diligently employed. Here and there he makes use of the Syriac. But the age of comparative philology, in the sense in which the term is now understood, had not yet arrived. The great scholars of the next sixty years, whose names are inseparably connected with Hebrew learning, as De Dieu, Pococke, and Castell (Castellus), rendered good service in preparing the way; but it was a hundred years before Schultens in Holland, by calling attention to the roots of Hebrew existing in Arabic, gave the impulse to the study of the cognate Semitic languages, which has resulted in the far more exact knowledge of the radical idea of Hebrew words which characterizes the lexicons of the present century.

The advantage gained by this wide and careful comparison of the cognate languages is, that instead of being dependent upon Rabbinic tradition, the interpreter is now able to test its correctness and expose its errors. He possesses the means of deciding, upon some solid foundation, between the divergent renderings of the ancient versions and on the probable meaning of the class of words which occur but once in the Hebrew Scriptures, and are therefore peculiarly difficult. The best results of the labors of Hebrew scholars for two centuries and a half in various directions and on a multitude of single points, gathered and presented in a compact form in the modern lexicons and grammars, place the interpreters of our day in possession of a mass of materials for forming a correct judgment on the meaning of the Sacred Text far beyond what was possible when the Authorized Version was made.

The bearing of this upon the character of the *modern versions* which we know were consulted is evident at a glance. These versions, of which several had been made into Latin, varying more or less from the Vulgate, represented simply the Hebrew learning of the time. The same remark is true of the translations made into the principal languages of Europe in the century which succeeded the Reformation. Selden relates in his *Table Talk* that "that part of the Bible was given to him who was most excellent in such a tongue, and then they met together and one read the translation, the rest holding in their hands some Bible either of the learned tongues, or French, Spanish, Italian, etc.; if they found any fault, they spoke, if not, he read on." With this agrees the statement in the original preface of the Authorized Version: "Neither did we think [it] much to consult the translators or commentators, Chaldee, Hebrew, Syriac, [New Testament] Greek or Latin, nor the Spanish, French, Italian or Dutch [German]." In availing themselves of these helps, in the way of comparison and suggestion, they acted wisely and well; but the testimony of the translations into the languages of modern Europe to which they refer would now be considered of limited value. One of the best of them, the Italian version of Diodati, which appeared in 1607, was issued in less than forty years in a revised edition. The version of Luther, which, in consequence of intwining itself into the language as well as the hearts of the German nation, has firmly held its place, is at last obliged, under the discovery of its numerous errors, to yield to the necessity of Revision. In Sweden, Denmark, and Holland the same necessity is found to exist, although in the latter country the States' Translation so called, made a few years after our Authorized Version, is one of high and undisputed excellence.

The *commentaries* on the Old Testament to which King James's translators were confined, aside from the Rabbinic expositions, were either those of the church fathers, who with few exceptions were wholly unacquainted with Hebrew, or those of the Reformers and their immediate successors. Many of the latter in their strong grasp of Christian truth and their vigorous exhibition of the thoughts of the sacred writers will always deserve to be studied. But on all questions of critical difficulty, on the decision of which not only the thought itself, but the whole connection so frequently depends, they were at a great disadvantage, and in numerous instances entirely missed the sense. Not one of them can now be used for the solution of a linguistic difficulty, nor be safely trusted, in many cases, to give the true thought of the original without the safeguard furnished by the more recent learned commentaries. This is said in no spirit of depreciation, but, on the contrary, with the highest regard for their work. But that work must be taken for what it was, and not for what it was not. The style and possibility of the highest critical commentary of the present day could only exist after the labors of successive generations of scholars on the ancient and modern versions, on the comparison of languages most nearly related to Hebrew, and on a multitude of subjects of critical investigation connected with the Old Testament. The results of these studies brought into a compressed form, and made to constitute a foundation for new and fuller explorations, constitute the peculiarity of the helps possessed by the interpreter of the present day, and indicate the necessarily narrower limits within which the scholars who prepared the translation of the Old Testament in our Authorized Version were restricted.

The nature of the *parallelism* found in the poetical books of the Old Testament was also less perfectly understood than at present, and the abundant contributions since made to the antiquities, natural history, and geography of the Scriptures now offer means for understanding many passages which, without this aid, could never be correctly interpreted.

SOME INACCURACIES OF THE AUTHORIZED VERSION OF THE OLD TESTAMENT.

BY JOSEPH PACKARD, D. D.,

Professor of Biblical Literature in the Protestant Episcopal Theological Seminary, Alexandria, Virginia.

As the more general subjects connected with the Revision of the Authorized Version have been sufficiently discussed, there remains only the more special subject of indisputable errors in our version, which need to be corrected. There is no better argument for revision, than the existence of such errors. If they could not be corrected, it would be unwise and unkind to make them known to those to whom the English Bible, and the English Bible only, is the Word of God. The only course to be pursued would be to hide them reverently, and thus not shake the faith of the unlearned.

We assume that the English translation of the Bible should be as faithful as possible to the inspired original, so that the unlearned reader may be as nearly as possible in the place of the learned one. There are some who practically deny this self-evident proposition. They would have us retain time-hallowed errors in our version; they appeal to popular prejudice. They remind us of the old priest in the reign of Henry VIII., who used to say, *Mumpsimus, Domine,* instead of *Sumpsimus,* and when remonstrated with, replied, "I am not going to change my old *mumpsimus* for your new fangled *sumpsimus.*"

While there is a wide spread opinion that our version contains errors, the only way to restore confidence in it is to appoint a committee of investigation to ascertain the exact state of the case. Even when no change is made the fact that examiners, in whom the Church has confidence, have found none necessary, must go far to inspire increased confidence. Isaac Walton tells us, "that Dr. Richard Kilbye, one of the Company of the Translators of the Authorized Version, heard accidentally a young preacher discussing the New Translation, and giving three reasons why a particular word should have been translated differently. The Doctor told him, on meeting him, that he and others had considered the three reasons mentioned, and found thirteen stronger ones for translating it as it was."

We proceed now to give some examples of errors in the English version, which are acknowledged to be such by the almost universal consent of critical commentators. The correction of these errors of translation will affect some texts often preached upon, and upon which a different interpretation has been put by tradition.

In the 24th chapter of Proverbs, 21st verse, we read, "My son, meddle not with them that are given to change." Now it happens that the word *given* belongs entirely to the English version, and is not found in the Hebrew, where the original word is a participial form, and means *changers*, or those *changing*. Matthew Henry says, "He does not say, with *them that change*, for there may be cause to change for the better; but *that are given to change*, that affect it, for change sake."

The English version of the book of Job has always been regarded by the best judges as very unsatisfactory. In Job iii, 3, where Job curses the day of his birth, he represents the night of his birth as saying, with joy, "There is a man child born!" Our version has it, *in which* it was said, thus destroying the poetic figure, which personifies the night. It should have been, Let the night perish, *which said.* In the sublime address of Jehovah to Job, in the 39th and 40th chapters, we find several verses in our version which fail to give the sense of the original. In the description of the war horse, chapter 39th and 24th verse, it is said, "Neither believeth he that it is the sound of the trumpet." If belief can be ascribed to a horse, it is the very thing which he believes, for he has heard the sound of the trumpet often enough before. The primary sense of the verb translated *believeth* is, *to be firm*, and adopting this we have this sense: Neither can he stand still at the sound of the trumpet. Virgil, in describing the war horse, says, "When the arms clash he knows not how to stand still."

In Job xl, 19, in the description of the hippopotamus, it is said in our version, "He that made him can make his sword to approach *unto him.*" The translation now almost universally adopted by the critics is, "His maker gives him his sword," or tusk.

In Job xl, 23, "Behold, he drinketh up a river, and hasteth not; he trusteth that he can draw up Jordan into his mouth." This gives no congruous sense. The translation adopted by Fürst, Conant and others, is—

"Lo a river swells, he is not afraid;
Fearless, though Jordan rushes to his mouth."

In Daniel ii, 5, "The king answered and said to the astrologers, The thing is gone from me." From the heading of the chapter, "Nebuchadnezzar forgetting his dream," etc., we infer that the Authorized Version understood by the *thing*, the dream, and that the king had forgotten his dream; but in that case it would not have troubled him. The true reason of the king's requiring them to tell the dream is given in verse 9th:

"Tell me the dream, and I shall know that ye can show me the interpretation thereof." The Chaldee word, translated in our version *thing*, is the same word, translated, verse 9, *word*, and also in chapter iii, 28, *the king's word*. It should then have been translated, The word has gone from me.

In Daniel vii, 9, "I beheld till the thrones were cast down," it should be exactly the reverse—were set up. So Gesenius, Fürst and others, as in Jeremiah i, 15: "They shall set every one his throne," or seat; and in Apocalypse iv, 2, "Behold, a throne was set in heaven."

In 1 Kings x, 28, in our translation it is said, "Solomon had horses brought out of Egypt, and linen yarn: the king's merchants received the linen yarn at a price." The context refers to the manner in which Solomon obtained horses by importation from Egypt. The word translated linen yarn is elsewhere translated gathering together, Gen. i, 10, and is applied in this verse to merchants and to horses. It should be translated, "And the company of the king's merchants fetched each *drove* at a price."

Much of force is lost in our translation by not observing the rule that where the same word occurs in the same context in the original it should be translated by the same word. There are so many cases where this rule is violated in our version that it is difficult to make a selection. In Isaiah xxviii, 15–19, where mention is made of "the overflowing scourge passing through," this is repeated four times in the original, with great emphasis. In our version the word translated pass through in verses 15, 18, is translated *goeth forth* in verse 19, and also *pass over*. The 20th verse would gain much in impression if translated, "As often as it passeth through it shall take you; for morning by morning shall it pass through, by day and by night." In the 17th verse our version makes judgment, or justice, not the measure, but the thing to be measured. The meaning is that God would deal in strict justice. "I will make judgment for a line and righteousness for a plumb line." In the 20th verse the translation might be improved, "For the bed is too short to stretch one's self, and the covering too narrow to wrap one's self."

The translation of the whole chapter is unsatisfactory. To go back to the first verses, the chapter opens with a woe denounced against Samaria, the capital of Ephraim, and alludes to its situation on a hill, at the head of a rich valley. "Woe to the crown of pride of the drunkards of Ephraim, and to the fading flower of his glorious beauty, which is on the head of the fat valley." Verse third: "The crown of pride of the drunkards of Ephraim shall be trodden under foot; and the fading flower of his glorious beauty, which is on the head of the fat valley, shall be as the first ripe fruit before the summer; which he that seeth, while it is yet in his hand, eateth up." If one will take the pains to compare the new translation of the fourth verse with the English version, he will see how much is gained.

In Isaiah vi, 13, our translation mistakes the meaning of the original. It contains a threatening of repeated judgment, but closes with a gracious promise, "And though there be left in it a tenth, it shall again be consumed; as a terebinth, and as an oak, whose trunk remaineth, when they are felled, so its trunk shall be a holy seed."

The space allowed us precludes the specification of any more passages, which might be greatly improved by a reverential and well considered revision, which shall amend the errors and supply the defects of our version. The lack of consistency in it, which cannot fail to strike every one engaged in the laborious yet most interesting task of unifying the translation of the same word in the original, wherever it occurs, and the sense permits it, will, we hope, be remedied by the Committee meeting in the same place. While the received interpretation of some texts may thus have to be given up, other texts, brought out into a new light, will take their place, and the gain will be greater than the loss. No one need fear that "the mingled tenderness and majesty, the Saxon simplicity, the preternatural grandeur" of our Authorized Version will suffer an eclipse in the Revision.

8

THE NEW TESTAMENT TEXT.

THE IMPERFECTION OF THE GREEK TEXT OF THE NEW TESTAMENT FROM WHICH OUR COMMON ENGLISH VERSION WAS MADE, AND OUR PRESENT RESOURCES FOR ITS CORRECTION.

BY PROF. EZRA ABBOT, D.D., LL.D., CAMBRIDGE, MASS.

It is an unquestionable fact that the Greek text of the New Testament from which our common English version was made contains many hundreds of errors which have affected the translation; and that in some cases whole verses, or even longer passages, in the common English Bible are spurious. This fact alone is sufficient to justify the demand for such a revision of the common version as shall remove these corruptions. Why, when so much pains is taken to obtain as correct a text as possible of ancient classical authors—of Homer, Plato, or Thucydides—should we be content with a text of the New Testament formed from a few modern manuscripts in the infancy of criticism, now that our means of improving it are increased a hundred-fold? Why should the mere mistakes of transcribers still be imposed upon unlearned readers as the words of evangelists and apostles, or even of our Lord himself?

The statements that have just been made require illustration and explanation, in order that the importance of these errors of the received text may not be exaggerated on the one hand or under-estimated on the other. We will consider, then—

I. THE NATURE AND EXTENT OF THE DIFFERENCES OF TEXT IN THE GREEK MANUSCRIPTS OF THE NEW TESTAMENT.—The manuscripts of the New Testament, like those of all other ancient writings, differ from one another in some readings of considerable interest and importance, and in a multitude of unimportant particulars, such as the spelling of certain words; the order of the words; the addition or omission of particles not affecting, or only slightly affecting, the sense; the insertion of words that would otherwise be understood; the substitution of a word or phrase for another synonymous with it; the use of different tenses of the same verb, or different cases of the same noun, where the variation is immaterial; and other points of no more consequence. The various readings which are comparatively important as affecting the sense consist, for the most part: (1) of the *substitution* of one word for another that closely resembles it in spelling or in pronunciation; (2) the *omission* of a clause or longer passage from *homœoteleuton,* that is, the fact that it ends with the same word or the same series of syllables as the one preceding it; and (3) the *addition* to the text of words which were originally written as a marginal note or gloss, or are supplied from a parallel passage. Ancient scribes, like modern printers, when very knowing, have often made mistakes while they thought they were correcting them; but there is little or no ground for believing that the text of the New Testament has suffered in any place from wilful corruption.

The state of the case will be made plainer by examples. The great majority of questions about the readings, so far as they affect the translation, are such as these: Whether we should read "Jesus Christ" or "Christ Jesus;" "the disciples" or "his disciples;" "and" for "but" or "now," and *vice versâ;* "Jesus said" or "he said;" "he said," or "he saith," or "he answered and said;" whether we should add or omit "and," or "but," or "for," or "therefore," the sense not being affected; whether we should read "God," or "Lord," or "Christ," in such phrases as "the word of God," or "of the Lord," or "of Christ;" these three words differing, as abbreviated in the Greek manuscripts, by only a single letter. Of the more important various readings, much the larger part consists of spurious *additions* to the text, not fraudulent, but originally written as marginal or interlinear notes, and afterward taken into the text by a very common and natural mistake. Most of these occur in the Gospels. For instance, "bless them that curse you, do good to them that hate you," is probably not genuine in Matt. v, 44, but was inserted in the manuscripts that contain it from the parallel passage in Luke vi, 27, 28. So the words "to repentance" are wanting in the best manuscripts in Matt. ix, 13 and Mark ii, 17, but were introduced into later copies from Luke v, 32.

For an example of *omission* from *homœoteleuton*, we may refer to 1 John ii, 23—"Whosoever denieth the Son, the same hath not the Father; but he that acknowledgeth the Son hath the Father also." Here, in our English Bibles, the last clause of the verse is printed in italics, as of doubtful genuineness. It is unquestionably genuine; how it was accidentally omitted in some manuscripts will be seen if we understand that in the original the order of the words is as follows: "he that acknowledgeth the Son hath also the Father," the ending being the same as that of the preceding clause. The copyist, glancing at the ending of the second clause, supposed he had written it, when, in fact, he had only written the first.

For an example of the *substitution* of a word for another resembling it in spelling, we may take Rev. i,

5, where for "*washed* us" (λούσαντι), the best manuscripts read "*loosed*," or "*released* us" (λύσαντι). For another, see the margin of the common version, Acts xiii, 18.

I will now give as full an account as is possible within moderate limits of the more important and remarkable various readings, that every one may see for himself to how much they amount.

The longer passages of which the genuineness is more or less questionable are the doxology in the Lord's Prayer, Matt. vi, 13; Matt. xvi, 2, 3, from "when" to "times" (most critics retain the words); xvii, 21; xviii, 11; xx, 16, last part (genuine in xxii, 14); xxi, 44; xxiii, 14; xxvii, 35 (from "that it might be fulfilled" to "lots"); Mark vi, 11, last sentence; vii, 16; ix, 44, 46; xi, 26; xv, 28; xvi, 9–20 (a peculiar and rather difficult question); Luke ix, 55, 56, from "and said" to "save them;" xvii, 36; xxii, 43, 44 (most critics retain the passage); xxiii, 17, 34, first sentence (most critics retain it); xxiv, 12, 40; John v, 3, 4, from "waiting" to "he had" inclusive (most critics reject this); vii, 53—viii, 11 (also rejected by most critics); xxi, 25 (retained by most critics); Acts viii, 37; ix, 5, 6, from "it is hard" to "unto him" (has no MS. authority; comp. xxvi, 14; xxii, 10); xv, 34; xxiv, 6–8, from "and would" to "unto thee;" xxviii, 29; Rom. xi, 6, second sentence; xvi, 24; 1 John v, 7, 8, from "in heaven" to "in earth," inclusive (the famous text of the Three Heavenly Witnesses, now rejected by common consent of scholars as an interpolation). Most of the questionable additions in the Gospels, it will be seen on examination, are from parallel passages, where the words are genuine; the doxology in the Lord's Prayer probably came in from the ancient liturgies (compare 1 Chron.

xxix, 11); the passage about the woman taken in adultery (John vii, 53—viii, 11), and some other additions, especially Luke ix, 55, 56; xxiii, 34 (if this is not genuine), are from early and probably authentic tradition.

Of questions relating to particular words or phrases, the following are some of the more interesting and important: Whether we should read in Matt. i, 25, "a son" or "her firstborn son" (compare Luke ii, 7); vi, 1, "alms" or "righteousness;" xi, 19, "children" or "works;" xix, 16, 17, "Good Teacher," and "callest thou me good," or "Teacher," and "askest thou me concerning what is good;" Mark i, 2, "in the prophets," or "in Isaiah the prophet;" ix, 23, "If thou canst believe," or simply, "If thou canst!" Luke ii, 14, "good will to [or "among"] men," or "among men of good will" (the latter expression meaning, probably, "men to whom God hath shown favor"); iv, 44, "Galilee" or "Judæa;" xiv, 5, "an ass or an ox," or "a son or an ox;" xxiii, 15, "I sent you to him" or "he sent him back to us;" xxiv, 51, omit "and was carried up into heaven;" John i, 18, read "the only begotten Son" or "only begotten God" (the words for "Son" and "God" differ in but a single letter in the old MSS.); iii, 13, omit "which is in heaven" (most critics retain the clause); vii, 8, read "not ... yet" or "not;" xiv, 14, "ask anything in my name," or "ask of me anything in my name;" Acts xi, 20, "Greeks" or "Hellenists;" xvi, 7, "the Spirit" or "the Spirit of Jesus;" xx, 28, "the church of God" or "the church of the Lord;" Rom. xiv, 10, "the judgment-seat of Christ" or "the judgment-seat of God;" 1 Cor. x, 9, "tempt Christ" or "tempt the Lord;" xiii, 3, "to be burned" or "that I may glory;" xv, 47, omit "the Lord;" 2 Cor. iv, 14, read "by Jesus" or "with Jesus;" Eph. iii, 9, omit "by Jesus Christ;" v, 9, read "the fruit of the Spirit" or "the fruit of the light;" v, 21, "the fear of God" or "the fear of Christ;" Col. ii, 2, "the mystery of God" or "the mystery of God, Christ" (comp. i, 27; there are several other readings); iii, 13, "Christ" or "the Lord;" 15, "the peace of God" or "the peace of Christ;" 1 Tim. iii, 16, "God was manifest" or "who" [or "He who"] was manifest" (manifested); 1 Pet. iii, 15, "the Lord God" or "the Lord Christ," or rather "Christ as Lord;" Jude 25, "the only wise God our Saviour" or "the only God our Saviour, through Jesus Christ our Lord;" Rev. i, 8, "the Lord" or "the Lord God;" iii, 2, "before God" or "before my God;" xxii, 14, "that do his commandments" or "that wash their robes."

I have sufficiently illustrated the nature of the differences in the text of the New Testament manuscripts; we will now consider their extent and importance. The *number* of the "various readings" frightens some innocent people, and figures largely in the writings of the more ignorant disbelievers in Christianity. "One hundred and fifty thousand various readings!" Must not these render the text of the New Testament wholly uncertain, and thus destroy the foundation of our faith?

The true state of the case is something like this. Of the 150,000 various readings, more or less, of the text of the Greek New Testament, we may, as Mr. Norton has remarked, dismiss nineteen-twentieths from consideration at once, as being obviously of such a character, or supported by so little authority, that no critic would regard them as having any claim to reception. This leaves, we will say, 7500. But of these, again, it will appear, on examination, that nineteen out of twenty are of no sort of consequence as affecting the sense; they relate to questions of orthography, or grammatical construction, or the order of words, or such other matters as have been mentioned above, in speaking of unimportant variations. They concern only the form of expression, not the essential meaning. This reduces the number to perhaps 400, which involve a difference of meaning, often very slight, or the omission or addition of a few words, sufficient to render them objects of some curiosity and interest, while a few exceptional cases among them may relatively be called important. But our critical helps are now so abundant, that in a very large majority of these more important questions of reading we are able to determine the true text with a good degree of confidence. What remains doubtful we can afford to leave doubtful. In all ancient writings there are passages in which the text cannot be settled with certainty; and the same is true of the interpretation.

I have referred above to all, or nearly all, of the cases in which the genuineness of a whole verse, or, very rarely, a longer passage, is more or less questionable; and I have given the most remarkable of the other readings of interest which present rival claims to acceptance. Their importance may be somewhat differently estimated by different persons. But it may be safely said that no Christian doctrine or duty rests on those portions of the text which are affected by differences in the manuscripts; still less is anything *essential* in Christianity touched by the various readings. They do, to be sure, affect the bearing of a few passages on the doctrine of the Trinity; but the truth or falsity of the doctrine by no means depends upon the reading of those passages.

The number of the various readings, which have been collected from more than five hundred manuscripts, more than a dozen ancient versions, and from the quotations in the writings of more than a hundred Christian fathers, only attests the abundance of our critical resources, which enable us now to settle the true text of the New Testament with a confidence and precision which are wholly unattainable in the case of the text of any Greek or Latin classical author. I say, enable us *now* to do this; for in the time of our translators of 1611 only a very small portion of our present critical helps was available. This leads us to consider—

II. THE IMPERFECTION OF THE GREEK TEXT ON WHICH OUR COMMON ENGLISH VERSION OF THE NEW TESTAMENT IS FOUNDED.—The principal editions of the Greek Testament which influenced, directly or indirectly, the text of the common version are those of Erasmus, five in number (1516-35); Robert Stephens (Estienne, Stephanus) of Paris and Geneva, four editions (1546-51); Beza, four editions in folio (1565-98), and five smaller editions (1565-1604); and the Complutensian Polyglot (1514, published in 1522). Without entering into minute details, it is enough to say that all these editions were founded on a small number of inferior and comparatively modern manuscripts, very imperfectly collated; and that they consequently contain a multitude of errors, which a comparison with older and better copies has since enabled us to discover and correct. It is true that Erasmus had one valuable manuscript of the Gospels, and Stephens two (D and L); Beza had also D of the Gospels and Acts, and D (the Clermont MS.) of the Pauline Epistles; but they made scarcely any use of them. The text of the common version appears to agree more nearly with that of the later editions of Beza than with any other; but Beza followed very closely Robert Stephens's edition of 1550, and Stephens's again was little more than a reprint of the fourth edition of Erasmus (1527). Erasmus used as the basis of his text in the Gospels an inferior MS. of the fifteenth century, and one of the thirteenth or fourteenth century in the Acts and Epistles. In the Revelation he had only an inaccurate transcript of a mutilated MS. (wanting the last six verses) of little value, the real and supposed defects of which he supplied by *translating* from the Latin Vulgate into Greek. Besides this, he had in all, for his later editions, three MSS. of the Gospels, four of the Acts and Catholic Epistles, and five of the Pauline Epistles, together with the text of the Aldine edition of 1518, and of the Complutensian Polyglot, both of little critical value. In select passages he had also collations of some other manuscripts. The result of the whole is, that in a considerable number of cases, not, to be sure, of great importance, the reading of the common English version is supported by *no known Greek manuscript whatever*, but rests on an error of Erasmus or Beza (*e. g.* Acts ix, 5, 6; Rom. vii, 6; 1 Pet. iii, 20; Rev. i, 9, 11; ii, 3, 20, 24; iii, 2; v, 10, 14; xv, 3; xvi, 5; xvii, 8, 16; xviii, 2, etc.); and it is safe to say that in more than a *thousand* instances fidelity to the true text now ascertained requires a change in the common version, though in most cases the change would be slight. But granting that not many of the changes required can be called important, still, in the case of writings so precious as those of the New Testament, every one must feel a strong desire to have the text freed as far as possible from later corruptions, and restored to its primitive purity. Such being the need, we will next consider—

III. OUR PRESENT RESOURCES FOR SETTLING THE TEXT.—Our manuscript materials for the correction of the text are far superior, both in point of number and antiquity, to those which we possess in the case of any ancient Greek classical author, with the exception, as regards antiquity, of a few fragments, as those of Philodemus, preserved in the Herculanean papyri. The cases are very few in which any MSS. of Greek classical authors have been found older than the ninth or tenth century. The oldest manuscript of Æschylus and Sophocles, that from which all the others are believed to have been copied, directly or indirectly, is of the tenth or eleventh century; the oldest manuscript of Euripides is of the twelfth. For the New Testament, on the other hand, we have manuscripts more or less complete, written in uncial or capital letters, and ranging from the fourth to the tenth century, of the Gospels 27, besides 30 small fragments; of the Acts and Catholic Epistles 10, besides 6 small fragments; of the Pauline Epistles 11, besides 9 small fragments; and of the Revelation 5. All of these have been most thoroughly collated, and the text of the most important of them has been published. One of these manuscripts, the Sinaitic, containing the whole of the New Testament, and another, the Vatican (B), containing much the larger part of it, were written as early probably as the middle of the fourth century; two others, the Alexandrine (A) and the Ephraem (C), belong to about the middle of the fifth; of which date are two more (Q and T), containing considerable portions of the Gospels. A very remarkable manuscript of the Gospels and Acts, the Cambridge manuscript, or Codex Bezæ, belongs to the sixth century, as do E of the Acts and D of the Pauline Epistles, also N, P, R, Z of the Gospels and H of the Epistles (fragmentary). I pass by a number of small but valuable fragments of the fifth and sixth centuries. As to the cursive MSS., ranging from the tenth century to the sixteenth, we have of the Gospels more than 600; of the Acts over 200; of the Pauline Epistles nearly 300; of the Revelation about 100, not reckoning the Lectionaries or MSS. containing the lessons from the Gospels, Acts, and Epistles read in the service of the church, of which there are more than 400. Of these cursive MSS. it is true that the great majority are of comparatively small value; and many have been imperfectly collated or only inspected. Some twenty or thirty of them, however, are of exceptional value—a few of very great value—for their agreement with the most ancient authorities.

But this is only a part of our critical materials. The *translations* of the New Testament, made at an early date for the benefit of Christian converts ignorant of Greek, and the very numerous *quotations* by a series of writers from the second century onward, represent the text current in widely separated regions of the Christian world, and are often of the highest importance in determining questions of reading. Many of these authorities go back to a date one or two centuries earlier than our oldest MSS. Of the ancient versions, the Old Latin and the Curetonian Syriac belong to the second century; the two Egyptian versions, the Coptic or Memphitic and the Sahidic or Thebaic, probably to the earlier part of the third: the Peshito Syriac in its present form perhaps to the beginning of the fourth; in the latter part of the same century we have the Gothic and the Latin Vulgate, and perhaps the Ethiopic; in the fifth century the Armenian and the Jerusalem Syriac; and in the sixth the Philoxenian Syriac, revised by Thomas of Harkel, A. D. 616, to say nothing of several later versions, as the Arabic and Slavonic.

Since the beginning of the present century thoroughly critical editions of the Greek Testament have been published by such scholars as Griesbach, Lachmann, Tischendorf, and Tregelles, in which the rich materials collected by generations of scholars have been used for the improvement of the text; we have learned how to estimate the comparative value of our authorities; the principles of textual criticism have been in a good measure settled: the more important questions in regard to the text have been discussed, and there has been a steadily growing agreement of the ablest critics in regard to them.

With this view of what has been done in the way of preparation, we will consider, finally—

IV. THE GROUND FOR EXPECTING A GREAT IMPROVEMENT IN THE TEXT FROM THE WORK NOW UNDERTAKEN BY THE BRITISH AND AMERICAN REVISION COMMITTEES.—On this little needs now to be said. We have seen that the text from which the common English version was made contains many known errors, and that our present means of correcting it are ample. The work of revision is in the hands of some of the best Christian scholars in England and America, and their duty to the Christian public is plain. The composition of the Committees, and the rules which they follow, are such that we may be sure that changes will not be made rashly; on the other hand we may be confident that the work will be done honestly and faithfully. When an important reading is clearly a mistake of copyists it will be fearlessly discarded; when it is doubtful, the doubtfulness will be noted in the margin; and the common English reader will at last have the benefit of the devoted labors of such scholars as Mill, Bengel, Wetstein,

Griesbach, Lachmann, Tischendorf, and Tregelles, who have contributed so much to the restoration of the text of the New Testament to its original purity. On the English Committee itself there are at least three men who deserve to be ranked with those I have named, Professor Westcott and Dr. Hort, two scholars of the very first class, who have been engaged more than twenty years in the preparation of a critical edition of the Greek Testament; and Dr. Scrivener, whose labors in the collation and publication of important manuscripts have earned the gratitude of all biblical students. Professor Lightfoot is another scholar of the highest eminence who has given much attention to the subject of textual criticism. We may rely upon it that such men as these, and such men as constitute the American Committee, whom I need not name, will not act hastily in a matter like this, and will not, on the other hand, "handle the word of God deceitfully," or suffer it to be adulterated, through a weak and short-sighted timidity.

One remark may be added. All statements about the action of the Revision Committees in regard to any particular passage are wholly premature and unauthorized, for this reason, if for no other, that their work is not yet ended. When the result of their labors shall be published, it will be strange if it does not meet with some ignorant and bigoted criticism; but I feel sure that all intelligent and fair-minded scholars will emphatically endorse the judgment of Dr. Westcott, expressed in the Preface to the second edition of his History of the English Bible (1872), "that in no parallel case have the readings of the original texts to be translated been discussed and determined with equal care, thoroughness, and candor."

INACCURACIES OF THE AUTHORIZED VERSION IN RESPECT OF GRAMMAR AND EXEGESIS.

BY REV. A. C. KENDRICK, D.D., LL.D.,
Professor of Greek in Rochester University, Rochester, N. Y.

Among the grounds urged for a revision of our version of the Scriptures are the imperfection of its critical text, obscurities growing out of changes in the language, and arbitrary variations in rendering, springing from the lack of fixed or correct principles of translation. Practically, however, the most important reason of all arises from the progress which, since 1611, has been made in grammatical and exegetical science, as applied to the Scriptures. That such progress should be made would be but to bring Biblical science into accordance with all the other developments of the last two centuries. In every field of intellectual action during that period, the progress of the human mind has been rapid, and its achievements unprecedentedly great. It would be strange, indeed, if in this highest of all departments of knowledge it should have failed of corresponding advancement. And it has not. In all the fields of sacred learning the most eminent abilities and the most conscientious industry have been diligently employed, and in none, perhaps, more than in the sphere of the language and interpretation of the New Testament. It is then no disparagement to the merits of those eminent scholars who gave us our excellent Authorized Version that their work in these respects demands revision. The fault was not of the individuals, but of the age. They lived near the borderland of a splendid realm of sacred discovery and knowledge, which it was not their privilege to enter. We might well take shame to ourselves, if, however individually inferior, we had not been thrown by the age itself somewhat beyond and above them.

Of course here, as in other branches of the general subject, we do not pretend that the errors which we point out are such as to pervert or darken the general teachings of the divine Word. The most that can be said of them is that they obscure individual passages, mar rhetorical symmetry, impede the flow of a narrative or the course of an argument, and sometimes seriously perplex the thoughtful reader, making him imagine the Bible to be a much less *consequential* and logical book than it actually is. Thus to give at this point a single illustration. In the opening of Hebrews, the writer sets forth the transcendent superiority of the Son to the angels from the vast disparity of their name and office. In illustration he cites from the Psalms: "Who maketh his angels [messengers] winds;" thus putting the angels on a level with the mere agencies of nature. This is perfectly clear. But the thoughtful reader, who reads in his Bible, "Who maketh his angels spirits," fails utterly to see the relevancy of a statement which in fact tends to give the angels the highest conceivable exaltation, putting them in essence on a level with the Deity.

From the same connection I will adduce another illustration. The author just before says, in latent contrast with the *stumbling* humbleness of the Son's earthly manifestation, "And when he shall again bring back into the world the first-begotten, he saith" (proleptic for, he will say), "Let all the angels of God worship him." But to him who reads, "And again, when he bringeth the first-begotten into the world, he saith," etc., the passage is an entire enigma. Christ's entrance into the world, at his birth from the Virgin, was one of humiliation. The angels undoubtedly *did* worship him, but it was no occasion for the formal challenging of that worship. The right translation throws it forward to the second coming, and brings all into harmony.

I. ERRORS IN THE USE OF THE GREEK ARTICLE.—But I proceed to take up the passages in some order, and will commence with illustrations of the use of the ARTICLE. The Greek definite article in many respects (not in all) squares precisely with the English. It cannot always be rendered, but it is no more used without a reason than is the English article. Yet, of its special use and importance, the English translators seem to have had but the faintest notion, and they render or omit it in the most capricious manner. "Into a mountain," "into a ship," appear almost constantly for "into *the* mountain," and "into *the* ship." "*The* [one] pinnacle of the temple" becomes "*a* pinnacle" (as if there were many). "A synagogue" stands for "*the* synagogue," which implies the only or the chief one in the place. Thus, Luke vii, 5, "He hath built us a synagogue," for "he himself built us our synagogue." The English version here contains three errors, "he" for "himself," "hath built" for "built" and "a" for "the," which, by a familiar idiom, we replace by "our." So Nicodemus (John iii, 10) is lowered from "*the* teacher of Israel," to which rank the Saviour exalts him, to "*a* teacher." In 2 Tim. iv, 7, "*the* good fight" (more exactly, "the noble contest," in contrast with the secular games of

Greece), becomes "*a* good fight," and "*the* crown of righteousness," which follows it, becomes "*a* crown of righteousness." In Heb. xi, 10, we have "*a* city that hath foundations," for "*the* city that hath *the* foundations," apparently of Rev. xxi, 19. On the other hand, the unwarranted insertion of the article in John iv, 27, "wondered that he was talking with *the* woman," instead of "*a* woman," quite changes the ground of the disciples' wonder. They knew nothing of the woman's history. Their surprise was that he talked thus at length and familiarly with a woman. So in 1 Tim. vi, 5, " their wives " should be simply " women." The apostle is speaking of deaconnesses, not of the wives of deacons. In 1 Tim. vi, 2, the force of the article with the participle is not recognized, and we have "because they are faithful and beloved, partakers of the benefit," for the apostle's appropriate and beautiful declaration, "because they that partake of their benefaction are faithful and beloved." In 1 Tim. vi, 5, by confusion of the subject and predicate we have "supposing that gain is godliness;" the original represents them as "supposing that godliness is [a source of] gain." In Rom. i, 17, and iii, 21, the definite article is unhappily introduced for "a righteousness of God;" seriously darkening the argument by the changed meaning thus forced upon the word "righteousness." But it is unfortunately omitted again in the striking description of John the Baptist, at John v, 35; "he was the lamp that was burning and shining." The English version here doubly errs both in the way of disparagement and of exaltation. Of exaltation, because it elevates to an original light him whom the Saviour designates as only a lamp, shining with borrowed brightness.

Of disparagement, in that it omits the emphatically repeated article by which Christ exalts John to a single and sole conspicuousness. He himself was " the light " (John i, 4), the fountain of all illumination. John was but a " lamp," shining as being shone upon; but still *the* lamp, that was lighted and shining. Again, the name *Christ* is in the Gospels invariably an official, not a personal designation. Here, therefore, the article should always be rendered: thus, " the Christ," viz., the predicted Anointed one.

I add one occasional misrendering of the article, produced by the influence of the Latin (which had no article), viz., " that " for " the." Thus in John i, 21, 25, we have " Art thou *that* prophet ? " for " Art thou the prophet ? " and the extremely clumsy, " If thou art not that Christ, nor Elias, neither that prophet," for " if thou are not the Christ, nor Elijah, nor the prophet." So in 2 Thess. ii, 5, 8, " the man of sin " and " the lawless one " become " *that* man of sin," and " *that* Wicked ; " while again, " the falling away," the definite apostasy, perhaps, of Matt. xxiv, 12, becomes simply " *a* falling away."

II. ERRORS IN PREPOSITIONS AND PARTICLES.—The PREPOSITIONS, in their variety and delicacy, are a most important element of the Greek language. In the rendering of these the Authorized Version is not unfrequently at fault, but its errors are so complicated by ambiguities in the use of English prepositions, that I shall not attempt to discuss them here. I will simply remark that it frequently confounds instrumental agency (*through* me) with ultimate agency (*by* me); and sometimes the instrumental (*through* me) with the causal (*because of* me). "*On behalf of*," at 2 Cor. v, 20, is turned to "instead of;" and at 2 Thess. ii, 1, it becomes "by." The preposition ἐν becomes needlessly sometimes "by," and sometimes "with." "On the clouds," at Matt. xxiv, 30, becomes "in the clouds;" and "on their hands," Matt. iv, 6, becomes "in their hands;" in both cases to the injury of the figure. Of all the examples here adduced that is the most important which obliterates the distinction between the ultimate agency of God (by) and the secondary agency (through) of his prophets, and even of Christ, as his commissioned one.

The PARTICLES are a no less delicate element of the language than the prepositions. The New Testament uses them but sparingly, yet, in the main, its use of them is thoroughly classical. In rendering these, also, our version is open to serious criticism. One of the simplest of them is the connective δέ, meaning strictly nothing but *and* and *but*, though *now*, as a quasi-rendering, is often a harmless accommodation to English idiom. Yet our English version renders it almost indifferently by *and*, *but*, *then*, *now*, *nevertheless*, *moreover*, *notwithstanding*, and when in the humor not to translate it, drops it altogether. In Matt. ii, 22, Joseph "was afraid to go thither, notwithstanding [for, *and*] being warned," etc. In Gal. ii, 20, we have the rendering, "I am crucified with Christ: nevertheless I live; yet not I, but Christ liveth in me." The elegant Greek runs thus: "I have been crucified with Christ, and no longer do *I* live, but Christ liveth in me." The particle μέν has mainly but one meaning, that of a concessive (not an emphatic) "indeed." The English often drops it, leaving its force to be given by intonation. In our version it is sometimes correctly given; sometimes by "truly," which approximates it; sometimes it is properly omitted; often omitted when its retention is important (Rom. vii, 25), and often rendered "verily," which strictly it never means. In Heb. ix, 1, "There belonged, indeed, now even to the first covenant;" the two particles are rendered "then verily," both of them being mistranslated.

III. ERRORS IN VERBS.—I pass to the VERBS. The errors here are of various kinds, and difficult to classify. I will mention first the frequent failure to distinguish between imperfect and absolute action. Thus in Matt. viii, 24, the ship was not "covered," but being or "becoming covered by (not *with*) the waves." In Mark iv, 37, the ship was not "filled," but "filling." In Luke iv, 6, the nets did not "break," but "were breaking." In Matt. xxv, 28, the lamps were not "gone out," but "going out." In Matt. ix, 2, they more picturesquely "were bringing," not "brought," "the paralytic." In Heb. xi, 17, Abraham, in the first instance (the verb is used twice in different tenses) "hath offered up," *i. e.*, he so stands recorded as having in purpose offered up his son; and then the writer, reverting to the actual scene, says, "and he that had received the promises *was offering* [had set out to offer] up," etc. The delicate distinctions of the two tenses are swallowed up in one common mistranslation ("offered") of them both. The force of the Greek imperfect it is by no means always best to try to reproduce; but it is often a pity to lose it. Thus in Matt. xxvi, 49, Judas "kissed" our Lord once, as indicated by the tense, but in Luke vii, 38, and in Acts xx, 37, the woman kissed repeatedly, "kept kissing" the feet of Jesus, and the anguished Ephesians the departing apostle. In Luke i, 59, the parents of the infant "were calling"— were about to call — but did not "call," his name Zachariah.

The Greek perfect tense is very uniform in its use, but is dealt with upon no fixed principle by our translators. They often confound it with the present, as Gal. ii, 20, "am crucified," for "have been crucified," Rom. v, 5, "is shed abroad," for "hath been shed abroad" (where the distinction is important). Rom. iii, 21, "is manifested," for "hath been manifested." It is quite as frequently, and more disadvantageously, confounded with the imperfect or aorist, as John i, 3, "was not anything made that was made," for "that hath been made." Matt. xix, 8, "from the beginning it was not so," for "it hath not been so." Matt. xxiv, 21, "Such as was not since the beginning of the world," for "such as hath not been from the beginning," etc. John iv, 38, "I sent you to reap," for "I have sent you to reap;" "others labored," for "others have labored." Heb. iv, 2, "Unto us was the gospel preached," for "hath the glad message been proclaimed" (*i. e.*, the promise of a rest); v. 3, "as he said," for "as he hath said;" v. 4, "for he spake," for "he hath spoken." Heb. ii, 3, "For this man was counted worthy," for "hath been counted worthy" (referring to his recent glorification). 1 Cor. xv, 12, "Be preached that he rose," for "hath arisen," or "hath been raised;" v. 21, "the first-fruits of them that slept," for "have fallen asleep," and hence, "are sleeping."

INCORRECT RENDERING OF THE AORIST.—I turn to instances of the incorrect rendering of the aorist. In its strict meaning (*I wrote, I spoke*), it is one of the simplest of the Greek tenses; its idiomatic uses, however, by which it sometimes represents our pluperfect, sometimes our perfect (growing simply out of a difference of conception), render it somewhat difficult to handle. Especially is it hard sometimes to decide whether it should be rendered strictly by our aorist, or more idiomatically by our perfect. But the authors of our version clearly have no fixed principle to guide them. As they often render the perfect as an aorist, so they often quite unnecessarily render the aorist as a perfect or a present. I take two or three examples from the Epistle to the Romans. Ch. v, 12, "all have sinned," for "all sinned;" vi, 2, "we that are dead to sin," for "we that died to sin;" v. 4, "have been buried with him," for "were buried with him;" v. 6, "our old man is crucified with him," for "was crucified with him" (ideally when he was crucified); v. 8, "now if we be dead with Christ," for "and if we died with Christ;" v. 17, "but ye have obeyed," for "but ye obeyed," viz., at your conversion; v. 19, "just as ye have presented," for "just as ye did present." Ch. vii, 4, "ye are become dead," for "ye were made dead," viz., when you were united with Christ. In 2 Cor. v, 4, we have "if one died for all, then were all dead," instead of "then did all die." The common version refers it to their previous death in sin; the correct version to their death in and with Christ *to* sin.

USE OF THE AORIST PARTICIPLE.—I give a few illustrations of the use of the aorist participle. It is well known that we have no exclusively aorist participle. We replace it primarily by our *present* participle used aoristically, then by our perfect, then by the finite verb. Thus the Greek ἰδὼν ἀπῆλθεν is either *seeing*, or *on seeing, he departed*, or *having seen he departed*, or *he saw and departed*. The Latin, which has neither aorist nor perfect active participle, very commonly resorts to the circumlocution, "*when he had seen he departed*." Our English translators have sometimes correctly adopted one or other of the first three renderings, but unfortunately have very often followed the Latin in a construction almost necessary in Latin, but not necessary and often clumsy in the English. For "calling together," they say "when he had called together;" for "entering the house," "when he had entered," and so in narrative very commonly. In many cases this gives an air of freedom to our version, and may as well be retained, as it probably will be in the present revision. Yet we have but to read, for example, the narrative portions of the Acts alongside of the original, to see how unfortunate is this continual Latin influence upon the naturalness of the diction of our English version. Take as a single and familiar specimen, Acts xxi, 3, "Now when we had discovered Cyprus, we left it on the left hand, and sailed," for "and coming in sight of Cyprus, and leaving it, etc., we sailed;" vs. 5, 6, "we prayed, and when we had taken our leave one of another," for "we prayed, and bade each other farewell;" v. 7, "and when we had finished our course from Tyre, we came," etc., for "but we, accomplishing (or having accomplished) our course," etc. In some instances the rendering involves serious misapprehension. Thus at Luke xxiii, 46, we have "and when Jesus had cried with a loud voice, he said, Father," etc., for "and Jesus, calling with a loud voice, said, Father." There is no good reason here for supposing that the crying or calling and the saying, are two distinct acts. Again, Acts v, 30, by reversal of the natural order, we have, "whom ye slew and hanged on a tree," for "whom ye hanged on a tree and slew." In Acts xix, 2, we have a mistranslation of both the aorist indicative and the participle: "Have ye received the Holy Ghost since ye believed?" for "did ye receive the Holy Ghost upon believing," or "when ye believed?" which is a very different idea.

IV. UNFORTUNATE RENDERINGS.—I shall now select a few farther examples of unfortunate renderings, without attempt at classification. The distinction between the indicative and subjunctive moods in conditional sentences ("if it *is*," and "if it *be*") is habitually neglected. Οἶδα, *I know*, (2 Cor. xii, 2,) is rendered *I knew*. Luke xxi, 19, "In your patience possess your souls," should be "in your endurance gain (*i. e.*, preserve) your souls." The verb to *become* (γίγνομαι) is habitually confounded with the verb *to be*, and sometimes improperly made passive. Thus, John i, 14, "The Word was made flesh," for "the Word became flesh." Heb. i, 4, "Being made so much better," for "becoming so much better," or "superior." Gal. iv, 5, "Made of a woman, made under law," for "born from a woman, coming under law." 2 Cor. iii, 7, "Was glorious," should be "came in glory." In Matt. xvii, 24, *seq.*, is an interesting account of an application to Peter to know whether his Master paid the "tribute-money," and our Lord's explanation to Peter why he should be exempted from paying it. The word in the Greek is entirely different from the ordinary word for the tribute or custom paid to the Roman government, and clearly designates the Jewish half-shekel paid to support the temple service. Yet, this distinction is lost in the translation. The reader has no clue to the special character of the tribute required, and the Saviour's beautiful plea for exemption, based on the fact that he was the Son of the Lord of the temple, becomes utterly unintelligible. "Tribute-money" should be "the half-shekel" (see Ex. xxx, 13). Again, in 1 Cor. ix, 26, 27, the apostle refers to the Grecian games of running and boxing. "I, therefore, so run as not uncertainly; I so box, as not beating the air; but I aim my blows at my body [literally, *hit my body under the eye*], and lead it in servitude." Here the generalizing of "box" into "fight," and of "aiming my blows at" (or "chastising") into "keep under," almost entirely obliterates the figure.

I give a few important examples from the Epistle to the Hebrews. Ch. iii, 16, "For some, when they had heard, did provoke: howbeit not all that came out of Egypt by Moses," for which read: "For who, when they heard, provoked him? Nay, did not all they that came out of Egypt through Moses?" Ch. iv, 6, 7: "Seeing therefore it remaineth that some must enter therein, and they to whom it was first preached entered not in because of unbelief: Again, he limiteth a certain day, saying in David, To-day, after so long a time; as it is said, To-day if ye will hear his voice, harden not your hearts." For this involved passage read: "Since, therefore, it remaineth that some enter therein, and they who formerly received the glad promise entered not in because of disobedience, he again fixeth a certain day, to-day, saying so long a time afterwards in David (as hath been said before), To-day, if ye shall hear his voice, harden not your hearts." At v. 9, the substitution of "rest" for "Sabbatic rest," takes the point out of the argument. At ch. v, 1, the rendering, "For every high-priest taken from among men," seems to select out a particular class of high-priests, viz., those taken from among men. The original, "For every high-priest, being taken from among men," points out, as a characteristic quality of the high-priest, that he is taken from among men. At ch. vii, 18, 19, is the rendering, "For there is verily a disannulling of the commandment going before for the weakness and unprofitableness thereof. For the law made nothing perfect, but the bringing in of a better hope *did*." For this read: "For there followeth an annulling of the preceding commandment because of its weakness and unprofitableness (for the law brought nothing to perfection), and the bringing in in its place of a better hope." I select yet one more example. The Greek denarius (δηνάριον) was worth about seventeen cents. Our version renders it by a "penny." When, therefore, the good Samaritan is made to take out two pence for his host, the English reader is not struck by his liberality. When the householder agrees with his workmen for a penny a day, they would seem to have better cause for murmuring than that the unequal labors are made equal in compensation. And when the angel flies through mid-heaven crying, "a measure of wheat for a penny" (in reality, less than a quart for seventeen cents), the English reader can hardly believe that he is not announcing extraordinary plenty instead of famine prices.

These examples of infelicities and errors in the Authorized Version have been taken almost at random, and might be indefinitely multiplied. They certainly are blemishes, but they only seriously mar, and by no means hopelessly deface, the structure of our magnificent version. They are spots on the glorious sun of our English embodiment of the divine Word. Thanks to God's gracious providence, these spots can not only be discerned by the telescope of knowledge, but with gentle hand can be taken away, causing it to shine with augmented brightness.

TRUE CONSERVATISM IN RESPECT TO CHANGES IN THE ENGLISH AND THE GREEK TEXT.

BY TIMOTHY DWIGHT, D.D.,
Professor of Sacred Literature, Department of Theology, Yale College, New Haven, Conn.

The Authorized English version of the New Testament and the Greek text on which it was founded have attained a sort of independent existence of their own. They have been accepted for so many generations as the true original and the accurate translation of the Sacred Books, that to multitudes of persons both in England and America there seems to be no doubt that they, and they only, are the Word of God. By reason of this fact the reviser of the English version finds himself, at the outset of his work, surrounded by a very strong conservative body, who are disposed to complain of and contend against every change. On the other hand, however, he discovers another party, who have not only freed themselves from the bondage of such views, but have become earnest for great alterations and improvements, or even for an entirely new translation. As these two bodies are irreconcilably opposed to each other, he is compelled to consider them both, and one of his first and most difficult questions is as to the plan which he shall adopt in his undertaking, with reference to their conflicting demands. To the consideration of the proper way of deciding this question, both with respect to the English text and the Greek, a few words may be suitably devoted in this series of articles.

I. In Regard to the English Text. If the work undertaken is to be a revision, and not a new translation, it can hardly be doubted that the style and vocabulary of the old version should not be altogether abandoned. It would seem, indeed, that this position is involved in the very determination to revise, and to proceed no further. But not only will this be admitted. It will also be held, as we believe, that, in the many changes which are necessarily introduced in the process of revision, it will be wiser and better to act upon conservative, than upon radical, principles, and even to err, if it be so, on the side of the former, rather than of the latter.

(1.) *The first reason* for this has reference to the success of the work in meeting the public approbation. The conservative party in this regard is much the most numerous section of the religious community, and, unless those who make up this section are to a reasonable extent satisfied, the revision cannot meet with general acceptance. They will cling to the old book, and the new one will soon be forgotten. However prudent it may be, in other cases, to disregard the probabilities of failure, it cannot be so here, for the years of labor will be almost wholly lost, unless the purpose with which they were entered upon shall be realized, namely, to introduce this revision into the place which has so long been occupied by the version of King James's time. Nor is this conservatism of the party alluded to an unreasonable one. The Bible, as it has been read for the last two hundred and fifty years, has so wrought itself in its individual words, and its general phraseology, and its sound as of sweet music, into the hearts and experience of Christian believers, that it must lose a part of its vital force, unless these are preserved. Any other book may be in the language of to-day, but this Book of books, which binds us to all the past and all the future, must speak to us not only with the same truths, but with the same sublime words, with which it spoke to our fathers.

(2.) *A second reason* for thus acting on conservative principles in respect to changes is founded in the fact, that the intermingling of modern words with the earlier ones is likely to destroy the harmony of the style, and may produce a worse result even than an entire remodelling of the whole after the usage of our own day would occasion. The great problem, indeed, which the reviser has to solve is how to bring in the new, without destroying the unity and beauty of the old. The fundamental rule on which the English and American companies are acting at present, is probably the best one which could be devised for the accomplishment of this end. It is, that where alterations are necessary they shall be expressed, as far as possible, in the language of the Authorized and earlier English versions. If the true meaning, that is, can be set forth by a word within the limits of the old vocabulary, it should be. But if it cannot be thus set forth, then faithfulness to the meaning requires that a new word shall be introduced. It is but natural, and the necessary result of the progress of our language during two centuries and a half, that it should have acquired the power of expressing by newly-formed words and phrases, or by new uses assigned to old ones, a clearer and more precise translation, in some cases, of what is found in the original Greek, than was possible in 1611. It must, surely, be the duty of the reviser to take knowledge and advantage of this fact, and to consider his obligation to give the reader the exact meaning of the sacred writer as paramount to everything else. If the word *self-control* will convey to the English reader the true meaning, in such passages as Gal. v, 23, Acts xxiv, 25, while *temperance*, by reason of its limited sense as now commonly used, is likely to be misunderstood; if *rational* gives more nearly the thought of Rom. xii, 1, than *reasonable;* if *anxious* in Luke x, 41, Phil. iv, 6, and similar cases, expresses the precise idea, and *careful* does not; if Paul means in Gal. v, 20, not *strife*, but *intriguings* or *caballings;* if the result which patience, or rather steadfast endurance, in tribulation works out, Rom. v, 4, is not *experience* but *approval*, or tested and approved character; if the uneducated reader or the child does not know that the *carriages* in Acts xxi, 15, were *baggage;* if the *prudent* spoken of in 1 Cor. i, 19, were *intelligent* or *sagacious*, rather than prudent; if Jesus and the disciples did not *sit down*, but *reclined* at the table at the Last Supper, according to the custom of the times; if the reader can be relieved from a frequent repetition of *howbeit*, by an occasional insertion of *however;* it ought not, in these and in numerous other and more illustrative cases, to be regarded as a sufficient objection to the words suggested, that they are not found within the limits of the vocabulary of the Authorized Version, or that some such words may even belong only to the language of a more modern era. But, even in these cases, the reviser should exercise every care and caution to select his words and phrases, if possible, so that they shall not break in harshly upon the harmony of the old style. One of his highest qualifications for his work will be shown by his success at this point; and in no respect, probably, will the new Revision, now in course of preparation, be more carefully scrutinized or more strictly judged than in this.

In the progress of time since our Authorized Version was published, an American language has, to some extent, come into being. Thoroughly English as we are in this regard, we have expressions peculiar to ourselves, which are no more provincial than the corresponding ones which prevail in the mother country. As the new Revision is for the English-speaking world, of whom forty millions are now, and one hundred millions soon will be, on this side of the ocean, it would seem that some regard should be paid to this American usage. Fortunately, however, there are only a few expressions, comparatively speaking, which can present themselves for consideration on this ground. The true principles to be adopted with respect to them would seem to be the following:

First, Wherever the one nation can readily understand the expression in common use with the other, but the latter cannot as readily understand that of the former, the one which will alone be comprehended by both should be chosen. Thus, for example, in Luke vi, 1 and the parallel passages, where Jesus is spoken of as going through the *corn-fields*, (which, according to our usage, means *grain-fields*,) the word should be left as in the Authorized Version, provided the English people understand by *grain* only that which is gathered in store-houses; but, if they also use this word in the same sense as ourselves, and refer it to what is in the fields, it should be changed to *grain-fields*, because *corn* with us has a special signification, which was not intended by the writer of the Gospel narrative.

Secondly, In cases where there is no such difficulty

of understanding the meaning of words, and yet there is a difference of usage, the form which will adapt itself most easily to both nations should be adopted. A comparatively unimportant example will illustrate this. The region designated, in Matt iv, 25, as *beyond Jordan* should be marked, in a new revision, as *beyond the Jordan*, because the latter form of expression is sufficiently in accordance with the usage of the English people, (although they have a provincial phrase corresponding with the former,) while, on the other hand, in America it is the only form which is ever employed.

Thirdly, In the representation, in the marginal notes, of the value of coins, this value should be expressed according to the money system of both nations. It would seem clear, that, if the ordinary English reader should be enlightened as to the relation between the Greek coins and his own, similar information should also be given to the American reader.

Fourthly, Mere provincialisms belonging to either of the two countries should be excluded. Thus the word translated *meat* in Matt. iii, 4, should be rendered *food*, because this is undoubtedly its true meaning, and because *meat*, as equivalent to *food*, is now, as Dr. Eadie states in his "History of the English Bible," a use of that word peculiar to Scotland. These principles and rules, indeed, may all be included in the general one, that a revision designed for the entire English-speaking world should employ such language as may best meet the wants of the whole body who make up that world.

II. IN REGARD TO THE GREEK TEXT. The principles which govern the work of revision here also should doubtless be conservative. Notwithstanding all that has been discovered and determined with reference to manuscripts and readings since 1611, it may be questioned whether we have as yet arrived at results which can be so generally established, to the satisfaction of all, as to render the formation of a universally received text throughout the New Testament possible. But, where the leading authorities in textual criticism are united, it can scarcely be regarded, at the present day, as unwise or improper to adopt the readings which they accept. Readings of this class, as every one can perceive, must have such weighty and preponderating evidence in their favor, as to commend them to the judgment of all unprejudiced persons. It will, also, be clear to those who have the means of investigating the subject, that there are cases, in which the leading authorities differ among themselves, where a determination as to the true text, and a decision favorable to a new reading, may safely be made. It will be better, however, to proceed with much care, and to introduce no change which cannot be very successfully defended, yet, in this department of the reviser's work, it is not essential that he should be as conservative as he is with regard to the English text. There are several reasons why it is not.

First, There is, of course, no such peculiar charm or influence connected with the style and sound, and music if so it may be called, of the original text, which has taken hold of every Christian mind, as is found in the language of the English version. Changes in the Greek may be introduced, here and there, or indeed frequently, if they are of a minor character, and yet, provided the general style and rhythm are preserved, there will be no grating on the ear or the mind.

Secondly, The prejudice of the conservative party in

favor of the old English text is more reasonable, than that which insists upon an unaltered Greek text. The Greek text on which our translation was founded, as every person of intelligence in this matter knows, was derived from a few manuscripts, mostly of secondary importance, and was prepared at a time when the greater part of the means which we now have at command was wholly unknown. The demand that no alterations shall be made in view of new evidence, which is brought by large numbers of new witnesses, and by witnesses of far more value than were previously examined, is one which would not be pressed in any other department of knowledge or life. It surely cannot be one which should be listened to in such a work as this. Nor will the Christian church, as it appreciates the facts of the case, justify the revisers in so far yielding to any who make this demand, as to refuse to introduce those alterations which ought to be adopted.

Thirdly, The proper determination of the Greek text is a matter more vitally connected with the precise thought of the sacred writers, than is the decision whether a word of the modern or of the earlier English style shall be used. The latter question may be one of comparatively little importance in many cases, but the former is one in which all Christians, whose earnest desire must be to know, so far as may be possible, exactly what the Evangelists and Apostles said, have the greatest interest. To settle this question according to the evidence at command, and with a conscientious regard for the facts of the case, which shall be overborne neither by any extreme conservative, nor by any excessively radical views, should be looked upon by the reviser as one of his chief duties.

Fourthly, In most cases, it is believed, it will be found that the changes which the weight of manuscript and other evidence will introduce into the Greek text, will bring out the thought more clearly and forcibly and felicitously. Setting aside the passages in which any doctrinal question may be involved, the presentation of a few examples of minor alterations, which are favored by prominent textual critics, will justify this statement.

In Matt. vi, 12, instead of *Forgive us our debts, as we forgive our debtors*, the reading should be, *as we also have forgiven our debtors;* the thought being, that the petitioner should not ask forgiveness for himself until he has already forgiven others. Matt. x, 23, *when they persecute you in this city, flee ye into another*, should read *flee ye into the next*, thus conveying not merely the idea of going to some other place, but to the next town, and so on until they had proclaimed the gospel everywhere. Mark i, 27, *What thing is this? what new doctrine is this? for with authority commandeth he even the unclean spirits, etc.*, should read, *What is this? a new teaching! with authority he commandeth even the unclean spirits, etc.*, thus expressing the astonishment of the beholders at the miracle, which they had seen, in a far more striking and more natural way. Mark ix, 22, 23, where the father, asking for the healing of his son, says, *If thou canst do any thing, have compassion on us, and help us*, the Authorized Version makes Jesus reply, *If thou canst believe, all things are possible to him that believeth*. But the approved text reads, *If thou canst! All things are possible to him that believeth*. The force of this form, which expresses surprise that the question of ability should arise, when to the believer everything is possible, cannot fail to be felt in comparison with that given in the old version. In Luke xv, 17 and 22, the naturalness and emphasis of the words are conspicuous in the additions of the modern text; where the prodigal, in contrasting his condition with that of his father's servants, says, *and I perish here with hunger*, (Authorized Version, *I perish*,) and the father calls to his attendants to *bring forth quickly* the best robe (Authorized Version, *bring forth*). Luke xxiii, 15, where the Authorized Version makes Pilate, after saying that he discovers no fault in Jesus, add, *No, nor yet Herod, for I sent you to him*, (the last clause being a mere parenthetical statement, not in the line of the main thought,) the change for the better, given by the new text, will be appreciated as it should be, *No, nor yet Herod, for he sent him back to us* — a proof that he also found nothing to condemn. In John x, 4 and 14, the slight alterations are improvements: *When he hath put forth all his own*, for *his own;* and, *I know my sheep and my sheep know me*, for *I know my sheep and am known of mine*, in which latter verse the parallelism with what follows is more clearly brought out, *Even as the Father knoweth me and I know the Father*. In Acts xviii, 5, it is more in accordance with the thought of the passage to read, Paul *was engrossed* or *wholly occupied with the word*, than, as in the Authorized Version, he *was pressed in the spirit*. Again, in Acts xxiii, 9, does not the verse gain a new force, if the scribes on the Pharisees' side are represented as saying, *We find no evil in this man: and what if a spirit hath spoken to him, or an angel!* instead of, as in the Authorized Version, *But if a spirit or an angel hath spoken to him, let us not fight against God*. In 1 Cor. vi, 20, the exhortation is more completely connected with the subject under discussion, and therefore is more impressive, if the words of the Authorized Version, *and in your spirit which are God's*, are omitted. The Apostle has been speaking *exclusively* of the body, and the best text makes him limit his exhortation to his converts accordingly, and call upon them to glorify God in their bodies. The somewhat obscure passage, 2 Cor. i, 20, is made clearer if we read, as we are authorized to do by the evidence in the case, *For how many soever are the promises of God, in him* (Christ) *is the yea,* (i. e. the confirmation of them;) *wherefore also through him is the Amen,* (i. e. the assent of the church,) *unto the glory of God through us.* Gal. v, 1, is more felicitously expressed by the modern text; *For freedom did Christ free us: stand fast therefore,* than in the Authorized Version, *stand fast, therefore, in the liberty with which Christ hath made us free.* In Heb. xii, 7, though some writers have held that the reading of the Authorized Version alone is intelligible, the careful reader will approve of the text as supported by the best authorities, *It is for chastisement that ye endure; God dealeth with you as with sons,* i. e. when you are called upon to endure sufferings patiently, it is as a parental discipline, and this discipline is the end which God has in view. And even in Rev. xxii, 14, where the strongest evidence is for the reading, *Blessed are they that wash their robes,* as against the Authorized Version, *that do his commandments,* it may fairly be questioned whether it does not present us with a finer and more natural thought, as it shows the author, at the close of his words respecting righteousness, turning back to the source of all true holy life, the blood of Jesus Christ. Other examples might be cited, which would be illustrative of the same point, but the limits of the present article will not allow their introduction, and those which have been adduced will be sufficient to establish what has been said.

Fifthly, In the cases, comparatively few in number, in which the state of the evidence indicates that words or sentences, whose loss will be a matter of regret, should be changed or omitted, the sound judgment of thinking men will decide that it is better to give up what does not have a true place in the Scriptures, than to retain it merely because we have become familiar with it, and dislike to see it no longer. For example, in Luke viii, 48, (where the question of insertion or omission is quite unimportant, since these words are certainly to be found in the parallel passage in Matthew,) the words, *be of good comfort*, may safely be omitted, because it can be made clear that the evidence against them is strongly preponderating. If the same fact can be established with regard to verses of far higher consequence, as those containing the doxology in the Lord's Prayer, Matt. vi, 13, or the statement respecting the descent of the angel at the pool of Bethesda, John v, 3, 4, or the story of the woman taken in adultery, John vii, 53 to viii, 11, or the concluding passage of Mark's Gospel, xvi, 9 to 20, it will, within a few years at the latest, and after the evidence has been candidly considered, be admitted that the rejection of them altogether, or the indication in some way of the condition of the case as it actually stands, is the right course to be taken. If, on the other hand, in these or other passages, the evidence is more evenly balanced, but yet is such as to make them doubtful, it will be held by candid men everywhere that the two possible readings ought to be given by the revisers; the one which they judge to be best supported, to be inserted in the text, and the other in the margin.

Sixthly, In the case of passages where different readings are found in the Greek text, and where, at the same time, doctrines are involved, the course which has just been alluded to must be the fair and proper one. Happily these passages are few in number, and they are not vital to the establishment of the doctrines; but, if the Revision does not deal honestly with them, it cannot satisfy the enlightened judgment of the Church. If the evidence in any particular case stands as ninety or ninety-nine to one against the genuineness of a verse, the verse in question should be treated accordingly. If it is but as fifty to forty, the Revised Version should give the translation of the better accredited reading in the text, and should add, in the margin, the alternate reading with some statement as to the degree of support which it can claim.

With respect to all these doubtful passages, and all those which clearly ought to be rejected, such changes may be introduced into the Greek text on which our Authorized Version was founded, as shall prove worthy of adoption either for the text or the margin of the new Revision, without violating the just demands of conservatism. On the other hand, no changes of a more sweeping character can be insisted upon by those who are not radical in an extreme and unworthy sense. The constitution of a body like the present Anglo-American Committee of Revisers, which represents both countries and many denominations, and the rules of which require a two-thirds vote for every alteration before it can be finally adopted, is the best guarantee that, in regard to the Greek text as well as the English, the progressive element will be sufficiently tempered and guided by the conservative, while the conservative will have the truly healthful influence of the progressive. By reason of this fact the success of the New Revision may be hoped for with great confidence.

THE GREEK VERB IN THE NEW TESTAMENT.

BY THE REV. MATTHEW B. RIDDLE, D.D.,
Professor of New Testament Exegesis in Theological Seminary, Hartford, Conn.

No revision can present to the English reader all the exact shades of meaning expressed by the voices, moods, and tenses of the Greek verb. This must be admitted at the outset. Yet in many cases greater accuracy can be secured. It is doubtful whether the true theory of the Greek tenses was accepted at the time the Authorized Version was made. It is certain that a great deal of ignorance still exists on this subject, even among those claiming some scholarship. If there be one point clearly established, it is that in Greek a writer used the aorist tense to express an action conceived of by him as momentary rather than continuous. Yet a long article in one of our prominent Reviews states that the aorist refers to past time of indefinite duration. This blunder arose from the fact that the name *aorist* means indefinite. But the indefiniteness of the tense consists mainly in its indefinite relation to other tenses, and not in its indefinite duration. Hence, the Greeks might express an action the most definite logically by this grammatically "indefinite" tense. This example of misapprehension may serve as preface to some remarks on the difficulty of reproducing the shades of thought expressed by the Greek verb.

I. The Greek verb has three voices, while the English has only two. It has one more mood than the English, but this one is of rare occurrence in the New Testament. The great difficulty lies in the fact that it not only has tenses for which the English forms furnish no exact equivalent, but tenses are carried into moods, and exist in participial forms altogether unknown to our grammar. It may be said that a Greek author had nearly twice as many forms at his command as we have, each having its distinctive use. This, of itself, presents a difficulty to the translator.

II. The difficulty is enhanced by another fact. The distinctions of the Greek verb, especially of the tenses, are not precisely identical with those of the English verb. A literal translation of a tense in the former language into one bearing the same name in the latter might be very inaccurate. The same is true of Greek and Latin, German and English. It is rare that two languages, even when they have the same number of tenses, present thereby the same distinctions. Just here, one who speaks a foreign language quite well, betrays himself most frequently before those "to the manner born." The Latin has fewer tenses than the Greek, and these not exactly equivalent to the corresponding Greek ones. Hence, the translators of the Authorized Version, like all the scholars of that period, frequently lost sight of the distinctions of the less familiar language, and used those of the Latin, which might, in the case of most of them, be called their second mother-tongue.

It will not be necessary to set forth in detail here the theory of the Greek tenses. Suffice it to say, that while the distinctions of past, present, and future appear in the indicative mood, there is combined with these a distinction of action, whether as continuous or momentary. In the non-indicative moods, the latter distinction is the preponderant one, often the sole one; as, for example, in the imperatives, present and aorist. The participles present the same distinction, but they are often only condensed statements of what might be expressed by the indicative. Hence, it is often difficult to determine whether an aorist participle is better translated by our English past or present participle, *i.e.*, whether it expresses an action antecedent to or synchronous with the leading verb. A mechanical student of Greek grammar has no difficulty here; as a school-boy he learned that τύψας meant "having struck," and so he regards all instances as equivalent to the English perfect participle. The most convenient distinction of tenses is that between the aorist and imperfect indicative—the former pointing to a past act viewed as momentary, the latter to a continued past action. But in the use of the imperfect there is generally a reference to some other action, up to which this "imperfect" action continued. Hence, the tense may express only the beginning of an action which was at once interrupted, or, on the other hand, may refer to an habitual or long-continued action. The perfect tense has no equivalent in English, since it refers to what took place in the past, and continues either as part of the same action, or as a result of it, up to the present time of the speaker or writer. Here we may use the English perfect or present, as seems most appropriate; but neither of them expresses all that is indicated by the Greek.

These distinctions are carried over into subjunctive, participial, and infinitive forms, and any one who bestows a moment's thought will see how difficult it is for us, with our English forms, to express such shades of thought. Then it will happen that, there being no exact English equivalent, two English forms will be equally accurate or inaccurate.

It will appear that it is no easy task to make a faithful translation, and also that there is little danger of any such excellence in the revision as will supersede the study of the Greek Testament.

III. It may be useful to note some examples where improvement seems both desirable and possible, as well as some where it is impossible. These might be indefinitely multiplied.

1. The Authorized Version, in hundreds of instances, renders the Greek *aorist* by the English perfect. This is almost always incorrect. The simple English past tense is well-nigh the exact equivalent of the aorist. In many cases, indeed, the meaning is scarcely altered by the more exact rendering, yet frequently the correction is of great moment. In Matt. i, 25, instead of "had brought forth," the Greek means "brought forth;" in ii, 2, "saw" should be substituted for "have seen." Every chapter of the Gospels probably contains an instance of this inaccuracy, which occasionally misleads. The use of "is dead" for "died" is allowable in Matt. ix, 24, and parallel passages, but in 2 Cor. v, 14, "then were all dead" leads to a misunderstanding of the passage; "then [or therefore] all died" is correct. In Rom. v, 12, "all have sinned," "have" is unnecessary and misleading. There is little need of citing other instances, for there is general agreement as to the correct English equivalent of the aorist.

2. In regard to the Greek *imperfect*, while its force is recognized by all scholars, there is great difficulty in determining when we ought to try and retain that force in English. We can say "he did this" or "he was doing this"—the former equivalent to the Greek aorist, and the latter to the Greek imperfect. Yet

the latter form is cumbrous, and if used constantly would seriously injure the style. Furthermore, even this form often fails to express the exact meaning of the Greek imperfect. In Luke v, 3, "was teaching" is more accurate than "taught," but it is not necessary to insist upon the change. In verse 7, however, "their net brake" is incorrect; the imperfect here means "began to break," though "their nets were breaking" is, perhaps, the best emendation. In verse 7, "began to sink" is the correct translation of a present infinitive, which has, in a subordinate clause, the general force of the imperfect. So in Matt. ii, 22, "was reigning" is the correct rendering of the present, according to the Greek conception of dependent tenses. In Matt. iii, 5, 6, the continued action is expressed by imperfects, but there seems no necessity for altering the English tenses, which here logically suggest this. In one class of passages the distinction between the aorist and imperfect is of importance, and yet can scarcely be reproduced. In the six accounts of the miracles of the feeding of the multitudes, the breaking of the bread is expressed by an aorist; but in four of the passages (Matt. xv, 36, correct reading Mark vi, 41, viii, 6; Luke ix, 16) the giving of it to the disciples is described by an imperfect, thus hinting that the Lord kept giving the broken bread as it multiplied in his hands. In these cases it would sound harsh to say either "kept giving" or "was giving." In Gal. i, 13, 23, 24, imperfects occur which occasion similar difficulty. Probably in more than half the cases the distinction cannot be recognized in a smooth translation.

3. The Greek *perfect* is properly a combination of the aorist and present, expressing past action with present

result. Hence, we must decide which element is predominant, and translate accordingly. In the common phrase, "as it is written," the perfect is used, and properly rendered by a present; but in Gal. ii, 20, "I am crucified with Christ," ought to be changed to "have been crucified," since the emphasis rests on the past rather than the present, both of them being included.

4. Passing to the non-indicative moods, we find that our forms do not, as a rule, express the distinctions of the Greek. The present and aorist subjunctive express respectively continued and momentary action, contingent on the leading clause, while our potential mood is not a subjunctive strictly, and by its tenses seeks to express past, present, and future time.

The imperatives are distinguished in the same way, but we must translate them all alike, leaving to the reader to determine whether the action commanded is once for all or continued. In Matt. v, 12, vi, 1, we have present imperatives, but in v, 16, 17, vi, 2, 3, we have the aorist. Further, the imperative in form is like the indicative, and it is difficult to decide which is meant. For example, John vi, 39, may mean "ye search the Scriptures" or "search the Scriptures," the context pointing to the former sense. In John xiv, 1, Matt. v, 48, and other passages, the same question arises. The infinitives present similar phenomena, but here there is opportunity for more exactness. The translation of the participles calls for great care. The present denotes continuous action, as a rule, and may be fairly rendered in English; but the combinations are such as to require skilful handling. The aorist participle has so often been incorrectly rendered by an English past participle, that this, and the corresponding misapprehension of the indicative, may be termed the chief blemishes of the Authorized Version as respects the verb. The cases where an emendation, either by the use of the present participle or by a change to the indicative structure, would be desirable, may be numbered by hundreds. The perfect participle is frequently used in the Greek Testament, but its sense cannot be exactly expressed in English except by a paraphrase, as in the case of the indicative.

5. The difference between "be" and "become" is expressed in Greek by two verbs, which are usually indiscriminately rendered "be" in the Authorized Version. In Matt. v, 45, we should read "that ye may become," etc. Similar cases to the number of sixty or seventy occur.

6. The middle voice in Greek has no equivalent in English. It is reflexive, and may sometimes be expressed by adding the pronouns *himself*, *themselves*, etc.; but no rule can be laid down.

It will appear from these remarks how numerous are the questions which come before the Revisers, how difficult many of them are from their minuteness. The effort has been to present to the New Testament Company every question however minute, and to discuss at least the possibility of expressing in English the shades of meaning recognized in the Greek. In one chapter of the Gospels, containing twenty-three verses, eleven emendations can be made involving the moods and tenses, probably half that number must be passed by. It may be estimated that greater accuracy can be secured in the vast majority of cases where the Authorized Version is faulty in its treatment of the Greek verb.

UNWARRANTED VERBAL DIFFERENCES AND AGREEMENTS IN THE ENGLISH VERSION.

BY PROF. J. HENRY THAYER, D.D.,
Andover Theological Seminary.

King James's translators, towards the close of their address "To the Reader," remark: "We have not tied ourselves to an uniformity of phrasing or to an identity of words. . . . That we should express the same notion in the same particular word, as for example, if we translate the Hebrew or Greek word once by *purpose*, never to call it *intent* . . . thus to mince the matter we thought to savour more of curiosity than wisdom . . ."

This decision to disregard verbal identity, provided the sense did not suffer, was a grave error. By translating the same word in the original by different English words, distinctions are inevitably suggested where they do not exist; on the other hand, by rendering different words in the original in one and the same way, differences in the sacred writers' thought are hidden from the modern reader. No sensible man, it is true, would think of making one word in English uniformly answer for each particular Greek or Hebrew term; nevertheless, in translating such a book as the Bible, the one supreme religious authority recognized by all Protestant Christians — in which, moreover, the change of a word may involve the change of a doctrine — the greatest pains should be taken neither to confound things which differ, nor to create differences where they do not exist.

Not that, with all our pains, it is possible always to

reproduce in a modern tongue the precise distinctions of the ancient. Languages differ in this respect; and even when the modern tongue is not, in general, inferior to the ancient in the capacity for nice discriminations, it will often deviate from it widely in those it actually makes. The distinctions, for example, which the Greek makes between the various words signifying *to know*, cannot well be reproduced in English. The evil spirit's reply to the sons of Sceva (Acts xix, 15,) might indeed be rendered, "Jesus I know and Paul *I am acquainted with,*" and our Lord's answer to Peter (John xiii, 7,) would be fairly represented by "What I do thou knowest not now, but thou shalt *understand* hereafter;" but it is not easy to mark the distinction in such passages as these: 1 Cor. ii, 11, "What man *knoweth* the things of a man, save the spirit of a man which is in him? even so the things of God *knoweth* no man, but the Spirit of God;" 2 Cor. v, 16, "Henceforth *know* we no man after the flesh: yea, though we *have known* Christ after the flesh, yet now henceforth *know* we him no more;" John xxi, 17, "Lord, thou *knowest* all things; thou *knowest* that I love thee." Or again, take the verbs denoting *to love:* the touching suggestiveness of the interchange of words in the threefold "Lovest thou me?" with its reply, in the passage last cited, must lie hidden from an English reader by reason of our poverty of speech; so, too, must the delicacy with which the Evangelist in chap. xi, after saying (ver. 3,) "Lord, behold, he whom thou *lovest* is sick," instinctively substitutes a less emotional term, when he comes (in ver. 5) to associate the name of Jesus prominently with the name of a woman: "Now Jesus *loved* Martha, and her sister, and Lazarus."

On the other hand, it must be confessed that our

occidental taste in matters of rhetoric—or rather our *English* taste, for it is doubtless traceable mainly to the influence of the blended Norman and Saxon elements in our language—makes us like a euphonious change in the phraseology, even when there is no change in the sense. Such passages as the following: Matt. xii, 5, 7, " Have ye not read how that . . . the priests . . . profane the Sabbath and are *blameless?* . . . But if ye had known what this meaneth . . . ye would not have condemned the *guiltless;*" Matt xxv, 32, " He shall *separate* them one from another, as a shepherd *divideth* his sheep from the goats ;" 1 Cor. xii, 4 *sq.*, " Now there are *diversities* of gifts, but the same Spirit. And there are *differences* of administrations, but," etc. ; Rev. xvii, 6, 7, " I *wondered* with great *admiration.* And the angel said unto me, Wherefore didst thou *marvel?*" Jas. ii, 2, 3, " If there come unto your assembly a man with a gold ring, in goodly *apparel*, and there come in also a poor man in vile *raiment;* and ye have respect to him that weareth the gay *clothing*," etc., most readers, looking merely at the *English*, would prefer to let stand as they are, rather than to substitute in each some single identical term for the words in italics, as conformity to the Greek requires. Yet, on consideration, we see that the biblical translator mistakes his duty, who compels even the ancient and oriental taste of his author to yield to that which is occidental and modern.

But our translators' disregard of verbal coincidences and variations involves what is far more important than any mere question of taste. Positive obscurities, amounting sometimes to unintelligibility, are due to it. What plain reader understands the saying (John xiii, 10), " He that is washed needeth not save to wash his feet, but is clean every whit"? Yet it becomes luminous when the sacred writer's change of terms is heeded: "He that hath *taken a bath* needeth not save to wash his feet [soiled even in coming from the water], but is clean every whit." What unlettered man is not thrown into perplexity when he reads, Matt. xxiii, 35, "of Zacharias son of Barachias, slain between the temple and the altar"? Was "the altar," then, not in "the temple"? The clue to extricate him from his perplexity is given him when the translator distinguishes —as the original author does—" *the sanctuary,*" or inner shrine, from "the temple," or sacred precincts as a whole. To many a child our Lord, in addressing (Luke xxiv, 25,) the two disciples on the way to Emmaus as "*Fools* and slow of heart to believe," has seemed to lie open to the judgment pronounced by himself (Matt. v, 22,) upon "Whosoever shall say to his brother, thou *fool*"— the verbal identity in English completely hiding from a childish vision the radical difference between the cases. Every reader, on the other hand, would naturally judge that Luke makes a far more sweeping statement than the preceding Evangelists, when he is represented as saying (xxiii, 44), "There was darkness over all the *earth,*" where they only use "*land.*"

And though this mistaken mode of translating may not often hide the meaning of the biblical language, it frequently blunts its point. That noteworthy declaration by Christ respecting himself (John viii, 58), "Before Abraham was, I am," gains greatly in force when the distinction between the passing nature of the former half of the statement and the permanence of the latter, marked in the Greek by the choice of two different verbs, is brought out in translation: "Before Abraham *came into being,* I am." Paul's reasoning in Rom. vii, 7, 8

—" I had not known *lust* except the law had said, Thou shalt not *covet*. But sin, taking occasion by the commandment, wrought in me all manner of *concupiscence*" —seems to an English reader to halt, when, had the translators but followed the apostle in describing the sin as it is described in the commandment, the sequence would have been as close in appearance as it is in fact: " I had not known *coveting* except the law had said, Thou shalt not *covet*. But sin... wrought in me all manner of *coveting*." The reiteration of " comfort " in the opening of the Second Epistle to the Corinthians has made many a believer's heart pulsate in blessed response; what a pity, then, that our translators wearied of the word sooner than the apostle did, who writes: " Blessed be God, even the Father of our Lord Jesus Christ, the Father of mercies and the God of all *comfort*, who *comforteth* us in all our tribulation, that we may be able to *comfort* them which are in any trouble by the *comfort* wherewith we ourselves are *comforted* of God. For as the sufferings of Christ abound in us, so our consolation [*comfort*] also aboundeth by Christ. And whether we be afflicted it is for your consolation [*comfort*] and salvation... or whether we be *comforted* it is for your consolation [*comfort*] and salvation... Knowing that as ye are partakers of the sufferings, so shall ye be also of the consolation [*comfort*]."

These infelicities are too numerous to be classified here. Our present limits will permit us only to enumerate—with the addition of an example or two by way of illustration—some of their unfortunate effects:

I. They are an impediment to the study of the Bible. For they deprive the student of the light often shed on the meaning of a word by its use in other passages, as exhibited in an English concordance. He comes, for instance, upon the word "atonement" in Rom. v, 11; and, so far as he can discover, it occurs nowhere else. But a correct translation would have enabled him to recognize the term made familiar elsewhere as "reconciliation." So in investigating the nature of biblical "hope," he is baffled by the fact that eighteen times out of thirty-two the translators have rendered the verb by "trust,"—thus virtually confounding the first two of Paul's triad of graces. And as respects the third, "charity," why should it be known by this name almost invariably in the First Epistle to the Corinthians, and have to be looked for under the heading "*love*" in more than fourscore instances elsewhere?

II. Again, they tend to conceal from the English reader delicate allusions and correspondences. No doubt the language in 1 Pet. iii, 14 as it stands — "If ye suffer for righteousness' sake, *happy* are ye"— prompts a reader to think that the apostle had our Lord's Beatitude in mind; but the allusion would have become indubitable, had the translators retained here the "*Blessed*" of Matt. v, 10. And who would imagine that the quotation given in Heb. iv, 3, "*As* I *have sworn* in my wrath, *If they shall* enter into my rest," agrees verbatim in the Greek with the quotation given just before (Heb. iii, 11), "*So* I *sware* in my wrath, *They shall not* enter into my rest;" while the hardly intelligible Hebrew idiom "*If they shall*" is rendered in the *Old* Testament, "*Surely they shall not.*"

III. Akin to the evil just mentioned is the obscurity thrown on some of the relations existing between the several parts of the sacred volume.

The Epistle to the Romans, for instance, has many points of verbal agreement with that to the Galatians, so has Ephesians with Colossians, 2 Peter with Jude;

but the English reader is hampered, in making such comparisons, by his uncertainty as to whether apparent agreements and differences are real or not. Does the Epistle to the Hebrews resemble in style the Epistles of Paul? The evidence of the best translations on such a point is necessarily inferior to that of the originals. But surely an English Bible student is entitled to a more truthful representation of the facts in the case than is afforded by the following parallel, in which the italicized words and phrases are all from the same Greek root:

"Thou hast *put* all things *in subjection* under his feet. For in that he *put* all *in subjection under* him, he left nothing that is not *put under* him. But now we see not yet all things *put under* him."—Heb. ii, 8.

"For he hath *put* all things under his feet; but when he saith, All things are *put under him*, it is manifest that he is excepted which did *put* all things *under* him. And when all things shall be *subdued unto* him, then shall the Son also himself be *subject unto* him that *put* all things *under* him, that God may be all in all."—1 Cor. xv, 27, 28.

Learned men are discussing the relation of the first three Gospels to each other, and to some common oral or written source. But how can we follow such discussions with our English Bibles, when verbally identical passages are made to differ as follows:

"Beware of the scribes, which *love* to *go* in long *clothing*, and love *salutations* in the *market-places*, and the *chief* seats in the synagogues, and the *uppermost* rooms at feasts: which devour widows' houses, and for a *pretence* make long prayers."—Mark xii, 38 *sq.*

"Beware of the scribes, which *desire* to *walk* in long *robes*, and love *greetings* in the *markets*, and the *highest* seats in the synagogues, and the *chief* rooms at feasts: which devour widows' houses, and for a *shew* make long prayers."—Luke xx, 46 *sq.*

We are not even put in a position always to judge correctly respecting the identity of the several incidents and discourses recorded by the different Evangelists. Surely our translators could not have had the fear of the modern Sunday-school superintendent before their eyes when they translated the Lord's Prayer in Matthew (vi, 10), " Thy will be done *in earth, as it is in heaven*," but in Luke (xi, 2), " Thy will be done *as in heaven, so in earth.*"

IV. Further, the translators' neglect of verbal discrimination hides in a measure from the English reader the individuality of the biblical writers. These writers may be recognized, as we recognize modern authors, by their favorite words and turns of expression. Take Mark, for example, who is sometimes represented as the mere epitomizer of Matthew and Luke; his personality as a writer manifests itself in a fondness for particular classes of words, yes, strikingly in the use of a single adverb—"immediately," or better, "straightway." So familiar a word is found, of course, in the other two writers; but it occurs in Mark nearly twice as often as in both the others put together. Yet so characteristic and simple a term as this has received five different renderings, viz., "straightway," "immediately," "forthwith," "anon," "as soon as," while elsewhere in the New Testament it is also translated "by and by" and "shortly." Still more numerous, and if possible more marked, are the words characteristic of John. Among them are the verbs *to abide* and *to bear witness.* Yet the former in our translation has seven different representatives, viz., *abide, remain, continue, tarry, dwell, endure, be present*—the first three being brought together in a single verse of the First Epistle (ii, 24); and the latter is translated *witness, bear wit-*

ness, bear record, testify, and (in the passive) *have good report.*

Paul's peculiarities as a writer are too salient not to stand out even in a translation which should take no pains to preserve them. The truthfulness of Paley's description of him, "off at a *word,*" is so generally recognized that the phrase has become proverbial. "Use this world as not abusing it," (1 Cor. vii, 31,) and other of his pointed sayings, have taken rank as popular maxims. His mental agility and adroitness in availing himself of the very language of opponents is now as piquant as a repartee, now as convincing as an argument. An oft-quoted instance, preserved by our translators, is that in Acts xxvi, 28, "Almost thou persuadest me," etc.; only it is to be regretted that they have chosen a translation which the Greek will not bear. But another instance on the same occasion they have seen fit to conceal. Paul's declaration, "I am not mad," is his dignified denial of the exact language of a charge which they have diluted into, "Thou art beside thyself," (Acts xxvi, 24.) Still less felicitously have they reproduced his retort to those at Athens who spoke of him as "a setter forth of strange gods." His allusion to this disparaging term is hidden, and again that to the inscription on the altar, "To an unknown god," is quite perverted by their rendering: "Whom therefore ye *ignorantly* worship, him *declare* I unto you."

V. But still more unfortunate is the translators' indifference to verbal agreements and variations when it affects matters of doctrine. Not often, probably, is a reader found so ignorant as to infer a difference of meaning from the change of rendering in Matt. xxv, 46, "These shall go away into *everlasting* punishment, but the righteous into life *eternal.*" But the confusion occasioned by translating "Hades" and "Gehenna" identically in every instance but one is not so harmless. The uniform transfer of the quasi-proper name "Devil," corresponding to the Hebrew "Satan," to those beings called "demons" by the original writers is also to be regretted. The unwarranted insertion of "should" in Acts ii, 47 (compare on the other hand, 1 Cor. i, 18; 2 Cor. ii, 15),— properly, " them that *were being* saved,"— has probably ceased to start false theological suggestions; but undoubtedly most readers understand the words of Christ to Bartimæus in Luke (xviii, 42), " Thy faith hath *saved* thee," to be of immeasurably higher import than the declaration in Mark (x, 52), " Thy faith hath *made* thee *whole.*" That the original term, indeed, may refer to spiritual healing is by no means impossible. In the case of the "woman which was a sinner" (Luke vii, 50), it clearly covers the forgiveness of sins. So that if it were a translator's design to intimate that the expression is *ambiguous* in the Greek, the variation in rendering would perhaps be allowable, provided in each case the alternate translation were given in the margin (as is actually done in Mark). In any event, however, the English reader should know that the language is the same in both Evangelists, and the same which is elsewhere (Matt. x, 22; Mark v, 34; Luke viii, 48,) commonly rendered, "Thy faith hath made thee whole." A single additional illustration: every reader of Paul knows the importance he attaches to the doctrine that "faith" is "reckoned as righteousness." But the proof-text from the Old Testament (Gen. xv, 6) on which the doctrine rests is given differently by our translation every time

Paul quotes it (Rom. iv, 3, compare ix, 22; Gal. iii, 6); and the verb itself, which may be called one of his technical theological terms, and which constitutes the very warp of his argument in Rom. iv, being used eleven times within the compass of twenty-two verses, receives there three different renderings.

Now, let it be repeated, that it is not always practicable to preserve identity of language in English where it exists in the original. *Sense* is more important than *sound*. The interests of the former, therefore, sometimes dictate the sacrifice of the latter. But it is evident that any fresh attempt at revision must proceed upon the opposite principle to that which was unfortunately adopted by King James's revisers.

ARCHAISMS, OR OBSOLETE AND UNUSUAL WORDS OR PHRASES, IN THE ENGLISH BIBLE.

BY REV. HOWARD CROSBY, D.D., LL.D.,
Chancellor of the University of New York.

The literature of a language serves to check its changes, but not to stop them. A living language must grow, and in the growth new words not only supply new ideas, but become substitutes for old words. The English of the fourteenth century had to be read with a glossary in the sixteenth century; but the three hundred years that have elapsed since Queen Elizabeth have not so altered the language as the preceding two centuries had done. The abundant literature of the latter period accounts for this difference, our English Bible of 1611 having probably had the most influence in this result.

It is not the archaisms of our English Bible which constitute the most important reason for a revised translation. Erroneous or obscure renderings form a far more conspicuous argument. But yet it is very true that there are many words and phrases in the received version which the ordinary reader would be likely to misunderstand, the words themselves having become obsolete, or their significations (or modes of spelling) having undergone a change. We append the following as specimens:

I. CHANGE IN SPELLING. — "The *fats* shall overflow with wine and oil" (Joel ii, 24), for "vats." "Lest he *hale* thee to the judge" (Luke xii, 58), for "haul," and "*hoised* up the mainsail to the wind" (Acts xxvii,

40), for "hoisted." "He overlaid their *chapiters* with gold" (Ex. xxxvi, 38), for "capitals." "And sat down *astonied*" (Ezra ix, 3), for "astonished." "*Or* ever the earth was" (Prov. viii, 23), for "ere." So we find *bewray* (betray), *magnifical* (magnificent), and *delicates* (delicacies). Many of these archaisms in spelling have been omitted in more modern editions of our version, as *leese* for "lose," *sith* for "since," *cloke* for "cloak." The old plural "hosen," however, still remains, in Dan. iii, 21, for "hose."

II. OBSOLETE WORDS.—"And they shall pass through it, hardly *bestead*" (Isa. viii, 21), for "served." "Besides that which *chapmen* and merchants brought" (2 Chron. ix, 14), for "market-men." "Old shoes and *clouted* upon their feet" (Josh. ix, 5); "took thence old cast *clouts*" (Jer. xxxviii, 11), for "patched" and "patches." "Neither is there any *daysman* betwixt us" (Job ix, 33), for "umpire." "Thou shalt make them to be set in *ouches* of gold" (Ex. xxviii, 11), for "sockets." "Doves *tabering* upon their breasts" (Nahum ii, 7), for "drumming." "The lion filled his dens with *ravin*" (Nahum ii, 12), for "plunder." "He made fifty *taches* of gold" (Ex. xxxvi, 13), for "catches." So *earing* (ploughing), *eschew* (shun), *habergeon* (coat of mail), *hough* (hamstring), *kine* (cows), and *leasing* (lying). We may add to these many of the names of animals, precious stones, etc., as *giercagle*, *ossifrage*, *behemoth*, *leviathan* (these last two being the Hebrew words untranslated), *sardius*, *ligure*, *bdellium*.

III. WORDS OBSOLETE IN THEIR SIGNIFICATIONS.— These are the most numerous and most important of Bible archaisms, because they are likely to be unnoticed, and the reader will thus form a wrong notion of the meaning of a statement. The manifest archaisms will always set one upon his guard, and lead him to investigate; but these words, having a perfectly familiar look, suggest no need of inquiry. Who would imagine that Ezekiel, saying, "as an *adamant*, harder than flint" (Ezek. iii, 9), and Zechariah, saying, "they made their hearts as an *adamant stone*," both referred to a " diamond "? The Hebrew word here translated "adamant" is translated "diamond" in Jer. xvii, 1. The *abjects*, in Ps. xxxv, 15, are the "dregs of the people." The *apothecary*, in Ex. xxx, 25, 35; xxxvii, 29, and Eccl. x. 1, is not our druggist, or preparer of medicines, but simply a "maker of unguents." *Aha*, in Ps. xxxv, 21, and many other places, is not an exclamation of one catching another in evil (as it now is used), but of one exulting over an enemy, and is equivalent to our "hurrah!" *Admired* and *admiration*, in 2 Thess. i, 10, Jude 16, and Rev. xvii, 6, have the old meaning of "wondered at" and "wonder," and not the modern one of delighted appreciation. *Affect*, in Gal. iv, 17, has the signification of "seek after zealously" (the Latin "affectare," rather than "afficere"). The passage means, "They seek after you, but not well; yea, they would shut you out from us, that ye might seek after them; but it is good to be sought after* always in a good thing." The Greek verb is ζηλόω, " to desire emulously," " to strive after." In Judges ix, 53, "*all to* brake his skull" is usually understood as if it were "all to break his skull," *i. e.*, "in order to break," whereas, "all to" is archaic for "thoroughly," or

---

* Perhaps the middle sense "to be impelled by zeal" is correct here.

"completely." *Atonement*, in the Old Testament, is the translation of the Hebrew "chopher," a ransom, or a cover for sins. See Ex. xxix, 36, and forty or fifty other places. But it really means "at-one-ment," or "reconciliation," the result of the ransom or cover. In the New Testament the word occurs only once (Rom. v, 11), where it means "reconciliation," (Greek, καταλλαγήν;) but this meaning is now obsolete. The modern *botch* is used exclusively for a clumsy patch or job; but in Deut. xxviii, 27, it means "ulcer." *Bravery*, in Isa. iii, 18, signifies "splendor." Who recognizes in the *camphire* of Solomon's Song i, 14 and iv, 13 (which suggests camphor!) the sweet-smelling "cypress"? and who imagines that the *caterpillar* of the Old Testament is a locust with wings? The *charger*, in Num. vii, 13 and Matt. xiv, 8, is a dish, and not a horse; the *ladder* of Gen. xxviii, 12 is a staircase; the *turtle* of Solomon's Song ii, 12, and Jer. viii, 7, is not a tortoise, but a dove; and the *nephews* of Jud. xii, 14; 1 Tim. v. 4; Job xviii, 19; Isa. xiv, 22, are grandsons. The *pommels* of 2 Chron. iv, 12 have nothing to do with saddles, but are "globes" resting on the summits of the columns. The word "quick" is almost always misunderstood in Ps. cxxiv, 3, "they had swallowed us up *quick*," as if it meant "rapidly." The passage means, "they had swallowed us up alive." *Prevent*, in Scripture means, "not prevent" (*i. e.*, anticipate), and *let* means "not let" (*i. e.*, hinder), so completely have these words turned over in signification. The latter is still used in law phrase as "hinder." *Deal*, in "tenth deal" (Ex. xxix, 40), means "part." *Outlandish*, in Neh. xiii, 26, means simply "foreign." Its modern meaning is "clownish." The *fenced* cities of Num. xxxii, 17, are "walled" cities, and the *hold* of Judges ix, 46; 1 Sam. xxii, 4, is a "stronghold." We use "peep" for the eyes almost altogether; but in Isa. viii, 19; x, 14, it is used of the mouth —"the wizards that *peep*." The same word is translated "chatter" in Isa. xxxviii, 14. *Intreat* (which with us means "beseech") is used for "treat," as in Gen. xii, 16. *Ensue* (French, *ensuivre*) is read in 1 Pet. iii, 11 for "pursue." *Evidently* and *comprehend* are now used of mental conditions, but in the Bible we find them used of physical conditions. "He saw in a vision *evidently*" (*i. e.*, clearly), Acts x, 3; "*comprehended* the dust of the earth in a measure" (*i. e.*, grasped), Isa. xl, 12; so John i, 5.

Conversation, in Scripture, never refers to speech, but always means "manner or course of life." Curious mistakes have been made even in the pulpit, by not observing this. *Comfort*, in the present use, signifies "soothing;" but in old English it had the force of the Latin *confortare*, and meant "strengthening." "Comfort one another with these words," in 1 Thess. iv, 18, is equal to "strengthen one another," etc. *Damn* and *damnation* are simply "condemn" and "condemnation," as in Rom. xiv, 23 and 1 Cor. xi, 29. "They shall *dote*," in Jer. l, 36, is "they shall become foolish." In Zech. i, 21, the carpenters came to *fray* the horns, and the reader supposes that this must mean "to plane" or "to saw;" but it means only "to frighten." *Honest* (Rom. xii, 17) and *honesty* (1 Tim. ii, 2) have not their present meanings, but are equivalent to our "honorable" and "honor." So *modest* (1 Tim. ii, 9) is our "moderate" or "seemly." *Unction*, in 1 John ii, 20, has the meaning of "anointing" (spiritually considered), while our modern use of unction is rather as "earnestness." *Vocation* (Eph. iv, 1) is the "calling" of God to be Christians, and not the trade or the occupation of life. *Go to* (as in James v, 1) is our modern "come," while "we do you to wit" (2 Cor. viii, 1) is the translation of two Greek words meaning, "we certify you." "We do you to wit" is, literally translated into modern English, "We make you to know." We might add another list of words whose signification has undergone a slight shade of change since King James's day, which the reader is almost sure to miss, but we have already surpassed our limits.

Since writing the above, Dr. Ezra Abbot has kindly sent me an additional list of examples, which I append.

1. *Changes in Spelling.* — In the edition of 1611 we find *aliant* or *alient* for *alien; clift* for *cleft; chaws* for *jaws; cise* for *size; fet* for *fetched* (very often); *flixe* for *flux* (Acts xxviii, 8); *grinne* for *gin; moe* for *more* (repeatedly); *ought* for *owed* (Matt. xviii, 24, 28; Luke vii, 41); *price* for *prize* (1 Cor. ix, 24; Phil. iii, 14); *rent* for *rend* (often); *then* for *than* (constantly); *utter* for *outer*.

2. *Obsolete Words.* — *Bolled* = swollen, podded for seed (Exod. ix, 31); *broided* = braided (*not* broidered), (1 Tim. ii, 9); *bruit* = report (Jer. x, 22; Nah. iii, 19); *neese, neesing* = sneeze, sneezing (2 Kings iv, 35; Job xli, 18).

3. *Words Obsolete in their Significations.* — *Artillery* = bow and arrows (1 Sam. xx, 40); *by and by* = immediately (Mark vi, 25; xiii, 21; Luke xvii, 7; xxi, 9); *careful* = anxious (Phil. iv, 6); *careless* = free from care (Judges xviii, 7; and so *carelessly*, Isa. xlvii, 8, etc.); *carriage* = baggage (1 Sam. xvii, 22; Isa. x, 28; Acts xxi, 15); *coasts* = borders, territory (very often), to fetch a *compass* (Acts xxviii, 13); set a *compass*

(Prov. viii, 27); *convince* = convict (John viii, 46; James ii, 9); *desire* = regret (Lat. *desiderare*), (2 Chron. xxi, 20); *discover* = uncover (often); *frankly* = freely (Luke vii, 42); *instant* = earnest and *instantly* = earnestly (Luke vii, 4); *liking* = condition (Job xxxix, 4); *with the manner* = in the act (Num. v, 13); *naughty* = applied to figs (Jer. xxiv, 2); *occupy* = use; deal in trade (Exod. xxxviii, 24; Judg. xvi, 11; Ezek. xxvii, 9, 16, 19, 21, 22; Luke xix, 13); *overrun* = outrun (2 Sam. xviii, 23); *painful*, not "distressing," but *hard, difficult* (Ps. lxxiii, 16); *proper* = beautiful, goodly (Heb. xi, 23); *purchase*, not "buy," but *gain, acquire* (1 Tim. iii, 13); *having in a readiness* = being ready (2 Cor. x, 6); *road* (make a road) = raid (1 Sam. xxvii, 10); *sometime* or *sometimes* = formerly; *suddenly* = hastily, rashly (1 Tim. v, 22); *take thought* = be anxious (1 Sam. ix, 5; Matt. vi, 25); *uppermost rooms* = highest or most honorable places (Matt. xxiii, 6); *usury* = interest (Matt. xxv, 27); *wealth* = weal, welfare (Ezra ix, 12; Esther x, 3; 1 Cor. x, 24); a *wealthy* place (Ps. lxvi, 12); the *wealthy* nation (Jer. xlix, 31); *worship* = honor (Luke xiv, 10); *witty* = wise, ingenious (Prov. viii, 12); *tree* = beam of wood, applied to a gallows, and especially to the cross. See the article *Tree* in the American edition of Smith's Bible Dictionary.

THE PROPER NAMES OF THE BIBLE.

BY REV. CHARLES A. AIKEN, D.D.,
Professor in the Theological Seminary at Princeton, N. J.

Any complete revision of our English version of the Scriptures must bring under review its proper names. The conservative spirit which is pledged in connection with the Anglo-American Revision now in progress, must protect them from unnecessary change. The question, therefore, is not, What alterations can be justified to scholars? but rather, What are needed in carrying out the proper and declared aims of the undertaking?

Unlearned readers of our Scriptures, if at all observant, encounter inconsistencies and are perplexed by obscurities that ought to be removed. Nor can it be regarded as a forced construction put upon the demands of "faithfulness," if, within proper limits, the names of persons, peoples, places, etc., be made to conform somewhat more closely to their original cast. Bible names are often significant; and piety may be helped as well as knowledge, when the religious idea embodied in many of these names is more clearly conveyed through the improved form given to them. If this work were an essay in "spelling reform," the attempt would be made to carry out a rigorously consistent system of transliteration, even though the reader might need a new introduction to *Jizchak* and *Ribhkah*, and many a family or locality besides. A smile would be very likely to greet *Binjamin*.

CHANGES IN PROPER NAMES.—In many cases the familiar proper names of our old version, and our

Biblical and Christian literature, will remain undisturbed, although scholars may be aware that this consonant and that vowel are not represented by an exact equivalent.

He would be unwise who would disturb names like *Abel, Job, Solomon, Balaam, Euphrates, Eve,* even though some of them may conform to the Greek of the LXX rather than to the more original Hebrew, and others to neither.

The general guiding principle should evidently be, that the Hebrew original ought to determine the form of Old Testament names, and the Greek that of names peculiar to the New Testament. Names common to both should consistently follow the older type. Exceptional treatment will be readily allowed in the case of names which are quite conspicuous and familiar in their present form in the Biblical narratives, and also in the case of those which have a common modern use. These it would not be wise to unsettle.

INCONSISTENCIES IN NAMES.—What changes are desirable? Plainly (1) *changes that remove inconsistencies* within the same Testament. When one word in the original is rendered by several different forms in the translation, the common reader is led astray. What is asserted of one person or place he understands of a number. When the familiar place *Gaza* is called *Azzah* in Deut. ii, 23; 1 Kings iv, 24; Jer. xxv, 20, the greater correctness of the form is no compensation for the loss of the identification; and for a place so well known the more familiar form should be retained. (There is room for difference of opinion as to the desirableness of using the margin to instruct common readers in such matters.) If in the New Testament the famous city of the Phœnicians might be called *Sidon*, after the Greek form of its name, there is no reason why in the Old Testament the otherwise uniform rendering *Zidon* should be abandoned in Gen. x, 15, 19. While double forms like *Abiah* and *Abijah*, *Uriah* and *Urijah*, may suggest that the Hebrew name has two different although closely related forms (from both of which the Greek form differs slightly), and while different forms of the name might be arbitrarily assigned to different persons, it only increases confusion when two forms are employed of the same person, *e. g.*, 1 Chron. iii, 10; 2 Chron. xii, 16, and 2 Kings xvi, 10; Isa. viii, 2. There is no apparent reason for describing the same person as *Enos* in Gen. v, and *Enosh* in 1 Chron i, 1, the form of the Hebrew name being the same in both cases; so with *Seth* and *Sheth*. There is nothing gained by calling the same man *Phuvah* in Gen. xlvi, 13, *Pua* in Num. xxvi, 23, and *Puah* in 1 Chron. vii, 1, although there may be two slightly different forms to the Hebrew name. It may be a convenience to have three forms, *Enoch*, *Henoch*, and *Hanoch*, to represent one Hebrew name as borne by four persons, but it is not helpful to have two of these forms applied to the same person (Gen. xxv, 4, and 1 Chron. i, 33). Common readers should be saved all occasion to ask whether *Jared* and *Jered*, *Gazer* and *Gezer*, *Phallu* and *Pallu*, *Pharez* and *Perez*, *Zerah* and *Zarah*, *Shelah* and *Salah*, are two names or one. The friendship of *David* and *Jonathan* has become proverbial and typical; why introduce the latter occasionally as *Jehonathan*, in rigid recognition of the fact that the Hebrew name has two forms? The same principle applies to *Joram* and *Jehoram*, and several other pairs of names. The *Cainan* of Gen. v and *Kenan* of 1 Chron. i are not understood by common readers to be the same name of the same person. *Ai* and *Hai*, *Uz* and *Huz*, are double forms, which if retained not only mislead, but chronicle an error.

The inconsistent treatment of forms like *Jidlaph* and *Jimnah* as compared with *Iscah* and *Ishbak*, or of *Jethro* and *Ithran*, is a matter of much less consequence; for here no confusion results. And yet whatever can be done quietly with inconspicuous names will justify itself to scholars with little disturbance to others. Linguistic or phonetic faithfulness is neither dishonor to the Word in its spirituality, nor excessive scrupulousness about its form. Yet such an endeavor should be cautious in its treatment of names conspicuous in the Biblical narratives; and all the more if from the Bible they have passed to any extent into our modern nomenclature.

There is, of course, no good reason why *Ishmeelite* should be conscientiously printed in Gen. xxxvii and xxxix, and in 1 Chron. ii, and the more correct *Ishmaelite* everywhere else; nor why *Zebulunite* should always be found in Num. xxvi, and *Zebulonite* in Judges xii.

In the New Testament there can be no advantage gained by perpetuating such double forms as *Noah* and *Noe*, *Sinai* and *Sina*, *Sodom* and *Sodoma*, *Canaan* and *Chanaan*, *Jeremias* and *Jeremy*, *Phenicia* and *Phenice* (with the additional reason in this case that *Phenice* is used in Acts xxvii, 12, to translate inaccurately another name). The common reader does not need to be told in the very text of his Bible how the Greek and Hebrew forms of such names may differ. Much less does he need to be drawn aside to think of the contrast between old English forms and the Hebrew and Greek.

HARMONIZING OF NAMES. — There may be room for more divided judgment in respect to (2) *changes that would harmonize the forms of proper names common to the two Testaments.* These discrepancies are usually due to differences between the Hebrew forms and those of the LXX and the New Testament Greek. Our version of the New Testament generally conforms its proper names in such cases to the Greek type. This is not, however, always done; *e. g.*, *David*, *Reuben*, *Issachar*, *Samson*, *Sarah*, and *Sodom* (except in Rom. ix, 29), are given in their familiar and not in their Greek form.

To the ends for which our version exists, what is contributed by disguising under a Grecian garb the names that have already become well known? Why introduce the patriarch *Judah* as *Judas* and *Juda*, or the prophet *Jonah* as *Jonas*? *Abijah*, *Ahaz*, and *Asher*, are well known; who are *Abia*, *Achaz*, and *Aser*? No help is given to "doctrine, reproof, correction, and instruction in righteousness," by confusing to common readers the identity of those whose words are quoted, or whose deeds and experiences are recorded. To preserve a more modern and unfamiliar form because it agrees better with the Greek, divides and weakens the unity and continuity of the impression which should be made by the two Testaments. The letter is honored at the expense of the substance. We would read still of *Hagar* and *Boaz* and *Gideon*, rather than of *Agar* and *Booz* and *Gedeon;* of *Haran* and *Canaan* and *Midian*, rather than of *Charran* and *Chanaan* and *Madian;* of *Shem* and *Terah* and *Nahor*, and not of *Sem*, *Thara*, and *Nachor*. If I read in the New Testament of *Methusaleh*, *Jephthah*, *Kish*, and *Uzziah*, instead of *Mathusala*, *Jephthae*, *Cis*, and *Ozias*, I should not be delayed in recalling what I know of them by the novelty of their names. *Elijah* and *Elisha, Isaiah, Jeremiah,* and *Hosea,* I know; with *Elias* and *Eliseus, Esaias, Jeremias,* and *Osee,* I must become acquainted. The lessons to be learned from the story of *Joshua* and of *Korah,* are often put out of mind when hidden behind the names of *Jesus* (Acts vii, 45, and Heb. iv, 8) and *Core* (Jude 11). To lose from our Bibles the names, *Ezekias, Jechonias, Josias, Urias, Zara, Sala, Saruch, Phalec, Phares, Roboam, Manasses, Joatham, Zabulon, Rachab,* if these were replaced by the old forms that never detain us to look at them as mere forms, would bring no real loss. And when to this list we add *Shechem, Zidon,* and *Zion,* in place of *Sychem, Sidon,* and *Sion,* the names that are common to the two Testaments are (unless something has escaped notice) all brought into correspondence.

Of the far more extended list of names peculiar to one or the other Testament, this brief paper cannot assume to speak exhaustively. Our object is secured if attention has been called to some of the ends to be aimed at in a revision of the proper names of the Bible, and some of the principles that should guide the attempt.

THE USE OF ITALICS IN THE ENGLISH BIBLE.

BY THOMAS CHASE, LL.D.,
President of Haverford College, Pa.

Few need be told that the italics in the English Bible — with the notable exception of a single passage — are used to show that the words so designated do not actually occur in the original Hebrew or Greek, and have been inserted because thought necessary either for the clear or for the idiomatic expression of the sense in English. The one exception is in 1 John ii, 23, where the last half of the verse was printed in a different letter, to indicate that it was omitted by some editors and (inferior) manuscripts; its genuineness, however, has since been established beyond question.

ORIGIN OF THE USE OF ITALICS.—While our Authorized Version has made probably a fuller and more consistent use of distinctive forms to indicate supplementary words than any other, it was not the first to adopt such a device. When Origen revised the Septuagint, he collated it throughout with the Hebrew, and wherever he found any words in the Greek to which there was nothing correspondent in the original, he marked them with an *obelos*, to denote their absence from the latter. Jerome used the same mark, for the same purpose, in his revision of the Old Testament in Latin, from the Septuagint. Sebastian Münster, who translated the Old Testament into Latin in 1534–5, distinguished by brackets such words, supplementary to those of the original, as he thought it necessary to introduce. Arias Montanus, in his Latin version founded on Pagninus, which was printed in the Antwerp Polyglot of 1569–72, marked all his variations from the Vulgate by italics. His course was followed by Beza, Tremellius and Junius, and other translators. The Spanish version of Cypriano de Valera (1602), and the Italian version of Diodati (1607), present supplementary words in a distinctive character.

Coverdale's Latin-English Testament (1538) shows intimations of distinguishing by brackets such words in the English as were in addition to the Latin; citing, in the epistle to the reader prefixed to the work, the authority of Jerome and Origen. In the "Great Bible" (1539) certain words are found in a type distinct from that of the main part of the volume, of which the Prologue gives the following explanation: "Whereas oftentimes ye shall find a small letter in the text, it signifieth that so much as is in the small letter doth abound, and is more in the common translation in Latin than is found either in the Hebrew or the Greek; which words and sentences we have added, not only to manifest the same unto you, but also to satisfy and content those that here before time have missed such sentences in the Bibles and New Testaments before set forth." The Geneva Bible was the first in English to use italics, which it employed on the same principles as our Authorized Version. The Bishops' Bible also distinguished supplementary words by a different character. Finally, in 1611, the first edition of our Authorized Version appeared, printed in black letter, with the supplementary words in Roman. When, in subsequent editions, Roman type was substituted for black letter, the additions were marked by italics, as they are printed at this day.

Only in the translation of a book in which each word is invested with momentous interest, could men have deemed it necessary to specify by a characteristic mark, words which are actually implied in the original, and omitted in it simply because not required by its idiom. If in the use of this mark our translators have erred, as I think they have, by excess, their motive deserves all praise. Even in cases where the words inserted are such as are plainly involved in the original expression, and indubitably necessary to set forth the same thought in English, they were unwilling to allow any term of their own introduction to go unlabeled, lest haply they might fail to give the reader due notice in some case where the necessity or propriety of the new word might possibly be open to dispute.

SUPERFLUOUS USE OF ITALICS. — Yet wherever, as in the majority of cases of italics in our English Bible, there is no room for doubt that the inserted words express nothing more and nothing other than the original text was meant to convey, it is superfluous to point them out. It is not the office of a translator to present information concerning the differences of grammar and idiom between the languages of the original text and the version; but it is his duty, availing himself of his own knowledge of these differences, to give his readers the clearest and directest statement in their own idiom of the precise thought expressed in the original sentence, without addition and without diminution.

The application of this principle would go far to clear our English Bible of those italics which to some degree strike the eye as blemishes. A very large part of them occur in some form of the verb "to be," especially in its use as a copula, a verb which the ancient languages omit readily; of similar frequency is the insertion by our translators of personal, possessive, or relative pronouns, indubitably implied in the original. Where there can be no doubt as to the precise form of the verb implied, or the pronoun to be used, it would seem unnecessary to designate the added words. Need the reader be informed of what is merely a difference of Hebrew and English idiom, by the italics in the sentence, "And God saw that *it was* good"? There is no necessity of italicizing *man* or *woman*, where the word is implied (if we may not say actually expressed) in the masculine or feminine terminations of adjectives, adjective pronouns, or participles; unless there be a possibility, in any case, that some order of being higher or lower than human is referred to, or that the distinction of man and boy, or girl and woman, might essentially affect the sense. It is being over-nice also to italicize the word *not*, after a preceding negative, as in Deut. xxxiii, 6; 1 Sam. ii, 3; Job iii, 11; xxx, 20, 25; Ps. lxxv. 5; xci, 5, 6; Isa. xxxviii, 18. It is simply a peculiarity of the Hebrew idiom not to require in such cases, as does the English, the repetition of the negative.

In addition to these whole classes of words, individual instances abound in which italics have been needlessly used to indicate words actually implied, or more than implied, in the original. Thus, in Luke xvi, 5, and several similar passages, "he called every one of his lord's debtors *unto him*," the preposition is in composition with the verb, and the pronoun is implied by the middle voice; in John xx, 5, 11, "stooping down, *and looking in*," "she stooped down, *and looked* into the sepulchre," the Greek verb denotes *look-*

ing as well as *stooping*, and should have been so translated also in Luke xxiv, 12; in such expressions as "the first *day* of the week," "the next *day*," "the *day* after," the word "day" is indubitably understood in the original, and is the only word that can possibly be used in English; in such phrases as, "hath not where to lay *his* head," "*thy* sins be forgiven," "lest they should see with *their* eyes," "we have Abraham to *our* father," "even as a hen gathereth her chickens under *her* wings," the possessive adjective pronouns are represented in Greek by the article, by a familiar idiom common to the Greek and various modern languages.

In some cases words inserted in italics are pleonastic, or simply superfluous. Thus, in Matt. iii, 15, "suffer *it to be so* now," *it* alone is sufficient; in Matt. xvi, 14, "some *say that thou art*," *say* would be better; in Luke iii, 5, "and the rough ways smooth" sounds better than "and the rough ways *shall be* made smooth;" in Luke xii, 58, "in the way" (that is, on the road), is enough without prefixing "*as thou art;*" in John viii, 6, the whole phrase, "*as though he heard them not*," is a gratuitous interpolation. In the following passages also the words in italics are unnecessarily added: Acts vii, 42, "*by the space of* forty years;" x, 29, "came I *unto you;*" xxiii, 22, "*see thou* tell no man;" Rom. xi, 4, "to *the image of* Baal;" 1 Cor. xiv, 3, "he that prophesieth speaketh unto men *to* edification;" xiv, 19, "yet in the church I had rather speak five words with my understanding, that *by my voice* I might teach others also, than ten thousand words in an *unknown* tongue;" xiv, 34, "but *they are commanded* to be under obedience;" xv, 41, "for *one* star differeth from *another* star in glory;" 2 Cor. iii, 3, "*forasmuch as ye are* manifestly declared to be the epistle of Christ;" Eph. iv, 14, "that we *henceforth* be no more children;" Heb. ix, 12, "having obtained eternal redemption *for us;*" 1 Pet. i, 22, "*see that ye* love one another;" 2 Pet. i, 21, "*as they were* moved by the Holy Ghost;" 1 John ii, 19, "they would *no doubt* have continued with us;" and Rev. ii, 25, "but that which ye have *already* hold fast till I come."

ITALICS INTRODUCED FROM FALSE INTERPRETATIONS.—There is another class of italicized passages, in which we can certainly find no fault with the translators for their designating the words which they have added, but modern scholarship discards the interpretation which they give of the sense of the original. Thus, in Ps. xix, 3, "*There is* no speech nor language, *where* their voice is not heard," the meaning is sadly perverted by the interpolations. Another notable example is in Heb. x, 38, "Now the just shall live by faith; but if *any man* draw back," etc. The proper translation is, "but if he draw back." The italicized words in John iii, 34, "God giveth not the Spirit by measure *unto him*," improperly limit the sense, and should be omitted. In Matt. xxv, 14, "For *the kingdom of heaven is* as a man travelling," etc., and in Mark xiii, 34, "*For the Son of man is* as a man taking a far journey," we should have *it is* in both cases; the meaning of "it," which is to be gathered from the context, not being correctly represented by the inserted words. In Matt. xx, 23, "but to sit on my right hand, and on my left, is not mine to give, but *it shall be given to them* for whom it is prepared of my Father," *it is for them* should be substituted for the italics of our translators. In Acts xxiii, 1, "Men *and* brethren" should be simply "Brethren" or "My brethren," the word translated "men" being used simply as a courteous prefix to "brethren." (The same word is used in the same manner at the beginning of the previous chapter, wrongly translated "Men, brethren, and fathers," as though *three* classes of persons were addressed, instead of "my brethren and fathers.") In Acts vii, 59, "calling upon *God*, and saying, Lord Jesus, receive my spirit," we should have "calling upon *the Lord*." Scholars may differ on the translation of Eccles. xii, 13, "for this *is* the whole *duty* of man," whether to accept our authorized version, or to say "for this *is* all of man," or "for this *is the duty* of every man." In 2 Tim. iii. 16, many prefer the interpretation adopted in some of the older English versions, "All Scripture given by inspiration of God *is* profitable also," etc. But whatever our judgment of the correctness or incorrectness of the view taken by the translators of 1611 of the meaning of any of these passages, they are good illustrations of the legitimate use of italics, as indicating words not *necessarily* implied in the original; and we cannot but commend the scrupulous honesty with which the reader has been notified in all such cases, and thus left free to adopt a different view of his own.

FELICITOUS USE OF ITALICS.—Instances of the correct and felicitous insertion of italicized words in the Bible are very numerous, and will be easily recognized by intelligent readers. Sometimes a slight addition promotes the smoothness and rhythmic flow of the sentence; thus the word *even* is often inserted, as in John xv. 26; Rom. iv, 17. In Ps. cix, 4, "For my love they are my adversaries, but I *give myself unto* prayer," the extreme conciseness of the original cannot be imitated advantageously in English, and the introduction of the new words is very happy. In a very few cases it might be an improvement to introduce italics where our Authorized Version gives us Roman letters; thus the italicizing of the word *it* in 1 Cor. xv. 44, would obviate a possible misconception of the meaning of the text, which reads literally, "A natural body is sown, a spiritual body is raised," or "*There* is sown a natural body, *there* is raised a spiritual body."

Revision of the Italics in our Version.—The italics in our Authorized Version have not been left without several revisions. The inconsistencies in their use in the edition of 1611, (or more properly in the use of the small Roman type which served the same purpose when the Bible was printed in black letter,) are not the least striking among the many indications of the haste and carelessness with which that edition was brought out. Thus in Hebrews x, 38, the words "any man" were printed in the same type as the rest of the verse. This oversight, with many others, was corrected in the carefully revised edition published at Cambridge, in 1638. Further modifications were made by Dr. Scattergood in 1683,* and particularly by Dr. Blayney, in the much esteemed Oxford edition of 1769, which he superintended. Dr. Adam Clarke, in his edition and commentary in 1810, complains of gross corruptions in the italics of Dr. Blayney's editions, "particularly where they have been changed for Roman characters, whereby words have been

---

* Also by Dr. Lloyd, in 1701, and Dr. Paris, in 1762. The typographical perfection of our Authorized Version, in conformity to its own standards, has been gradually achieved by the patient labor of many hands.

attributed to God which he never spake," and introduces many "corrections." Dr. Scrivener, in his Cambridge Paragraph Bible of 1870, has endeavored to make the use of italics uniform and consistent; a work in which he found, as he says in his preface, that "not a little remained to be accomplished."

I have already intimated my own opinion that some of the italicized words in our English Bible are gratuitous interpolations, and that a very considerable reduction may be made in the remaining number without depriving the reader of any information concerning the original text which would be of real value to him. But the question of their retention or dismissal is sometimes a delicate one; and wherever it is not easy to decide that they are of no use, they should have the benefit of the doubt.

PARAGRAPHS, CHAPTERS, AND VERSES OF THE BIBLE.

BY PROFESSOR JAMES STRONG, S.T.D.,
Of Drew Theological Seminary, N. J.

THE DIVISION OF THE BIBLE into chapters originated with the commentators of the Middle Ages as a convenience. Cardinal Hugh, of St. Cher, adopted it in his Concordance to the Latin Vulgate, about A. D. 1244, and it was thence transferred to the Hebrew and Greek originals. The division into verses, in the Old Testament, is found in the Hebrew manuscripts of the earliest date. In the New Testament it was hastily made by the printer, Robert Stephens, for the third edition of his Greek Testament, published in 1551. The chapters and verses in the common English Bible differ in but a few places from those now generally indicated in the printed editions of the Hebrew and Greek texts. They constitute the paragraph marks or breaks in the lines in King James's version. In the Hebrew Bible, however, the numerals for the chapters and verses are placed in the margin, and the text is broken into large sections for the synagogue lessons, and smaller ones of a more arbitrary character. This has been partly imitated in some editions of the English Bible, by placing a paragraph mark (¶) at the head of verses supposed to begin a new subject; but in neither case has the division been convenient, uniform, or logical. In the original edition (1611) of the Authorized Version this mark is prefixed, in the Psalms, to the special titles only; in the other books it is interspersed most capriciously. In the new Anglo-American revision the marks of chapter and verse will be retained for reference; but the text will be divided into sections, on some plan not yet fully settled. It is earnestly hoped that neither the Masoretic nor any other conventional mode of division will be implicitly followed, but that the paragraphs will correctly indicate the changes of topics. The *parallelism* in the poetical books will be shown by printing in verse-form, which will be an immense gain in the clearness and force of meaning. For example, the earliest specimen of poetry extant (Gen. iv, 23, 24) illustrates itself if arranged in some such way as this:

"And Lamech said unto his wives,
   Adah and Zillah,   Hear my voice;
  Ye wives of Lamech, Hearken unto my speech:
    For I have slain a man to my wounding,
    And a young man to my hurt.
      If Cain shall be avenged sevenfold,
      Truly Lamech seventy and sevenfold."

CHAPTER AND VERSE DIVISIONS. — The present division into chapters and verses is manifestly injudicious, and some of the advantages of a just paragraph system are the following, which we will illustrate by a few examples:

1. *The sense is greatly injured by the one method, and improved by the other.* — Oftentimes the closest connection of thought is broken up by the present division, which is purely accidental; and, *vice versa*, a connection is falsely suggested where there is really a break in the subject. Thus, at the very outset, the account of the general creation, in Gen. i, properly includes verses 1–3 of Chapter ii, as every indication in the text shows; while verse 4 begins the narrative of man's trial in Eden. So, in the last chapter of Revelation, verses 1–5 belong to the description of the heavenly city preced-

ing, and the remaining verses contain an entirely distinct topic. Similar instances are innumerable, as any judiciously arranged "Paragraph Bible" will show. In like manner, the verses frequently interrupt a sentence, sometimes very strangely, as in Ps. xcviii, 8, 9, " Let the hills be joyful together — before the Lord;" and so Ps. xcvi, 12, 13. The mere fact of beginning a new verse with a capital letter, after a comma, or some other of the lesser punctuation marks, is calculated to mislead the reader, and induce a defective and erroneous habit of quoting Scripture. Probably this has been a fruitful cause of the prevalent practice of perverting proof-texts, by neglecting the context. On the contrary, how much more beautiful would the description of charity, in 1 Cor. xiii, become if read in immediate connection, as exemplifying the " more excellent way" of the last verse of the preceding chapter, and as enforcing the exhortation to " follow after charity," in the first verse of the following chapter. Proper paragraphing is a sort of analysis of a book or chapter, so as to be evident at a glance. How would a modern history, or poem, or epistle look, if the printer should chop it up in the fashion of our common Bibles? It greatly impairs the significance and dignity of the sacred volume.

2. *The present arrangement is a loss in every respect.*— For convenience of consultation the verse and chapter numbers are certainly preferable in the margin, where the eye can rapidly run down them in single file. There is surely no economy of space in losing part of a line at the end of nearly every verse. There is little beauty in the ragged-looking page that these frequent and irregular blanks make. The double columns which this method of typography almost necessitates shorten

the measure and destroy uniformity of spacing. There is small comfort in reading at one time a chapter, sometimes unduly long, sometimes very short, without being sure that you have the whole subject together. Finally, on the ordinary plan, it is impossible to distinguish the poetical from the prose portions of the Bible. All these things considered, it is a wonder that intelligent readers will tolerate the chapter-and-verse mode of paragraphing. Nothing but slavery to custom could reconcile us to it in these days of literary and mechanical improvement.

REVISION OF THE SCRIPTURES.

BY THE RIGHT REV. ALFRED LEE.

"He that hath my word, let him speak my word faithfully." — JER. xxiii, 28.

OBJECTIONS TO A REVISION.—That the proposal to set forth a revision of the English Bible should awaken opposition and distrust, will surprise no one who has given the least reflection to the subject, or who is conversant with the history of the sacred text. In proportion to the value set upon this version will be the anxiety and alarm at the suggestion of change. To the great majority of readers the Bible to which they have been always accustomed is the word of God, *verbatim et literatim*. Accepting all Scripture as given by inspiration of God, they have been wont to regard every syllable with equal veneration. The words and phrases, associated in memory with the happiest and most solemn hours of their lives, are redolent of that heaven from which they are supposed to come, and to part with the smallest fragment is a most painful thought. The devout reader feels as if he were to be robbed of that which is more precious than gold.

Very many, who value their Bible above all price, scarcely ever remember that what they have before their eyes is not the very utterance of men moved by the Holy Ghost, but a translation from other languages, and so far, a human work. As a human work it is liable to the error and imperfection incident to whatever is human. So also, as committed to writing, it has during many ages been exposed to suffer from errors of transcribers, and even endeavors well meant, however mistaken, to correct and improve the original. The impression has been cherished and common that the Holy One who gave men his word has interposed, by perpetual miracle, to guard it from alteration or corruption. So that infallibility has been virtually attributed not only to the prophets, apostles and evangelists who wrote the different books, but to scribes, copyists and translators, through whom they have been handed down to us.

Now while we gratefully acknowledge the providence of Almighty God, in preserving and watching over these communications of his will, so that we have a sure and sufficient rule of faith and practice, it is undeniable that no such miracle has been wrought. Scribes and translators have not been exempt from human infirmities. Errors have crept into the text, sometimes from design, oftener from accident.

Our English Bible, commonly known as the Authorized Version, with all its claims upon our reverence and confidence, does not contain the lively oracles as originally spoken or recorded. It is God's word only so far as the primal text has been exactly preserved and faithfully rendered into our tongue. To admit this is to cast no reflection upon the work itself, or upon those who were engaged in its preparation. All honor to the noble band of Christian scholars who, from Wickliffe down to the revisers appointed by King James, labored to present the Holy Scriptures in the English language. Many of them died for their loyalty and devotion to the truth which they sought to diffuse. All of them were men eminent for learning, as for purity and holiness of life. They left behind them a monument enduring and admirable. The very comparison of the dates 1611 and 1870 is an emphatic witness to the high qualifications and conscientious fidelity of those last named. For more than two centuries and a half their revision has held its place, gathering around it the affections of the great mass of those who speak the English tongue, and the homage and admiration of the learned. No eulogistic language has seemed to overpass its merits. And those who promote and encourage the revision now in progress, as well as those actually participating in the work, yield to none in sincere and enlightened appreciation of the excellences of the Authorized Version.

ADVANCES IN TEXTUAL CRITICISM.—But the world has not been standing still since 1611, and among other advances, prodigious strides have been made in branches of knowledge bearing upon the right understanding of the Holy Scriptures. Textual criticism has so improved as to be almost ranked as a new science. Men of varied acquirements, and of the richest intellectual gifts, have given years to the patient investigation of the subject. Diligent exploration has brought to light ancient manuscripts of inestimable worth. Every word and letter has been examined with scrupulous and painstaking care. Of the extent and thoroughness of these researches and studies, one who has not examined the subject can have little conception. And while the materials have thus been collected from all sources, the knowledge of the languages in which the Scriptures were written has been greatly enlarged and perfected. This is specially true of Greek scholarship. Apart from striking and obvious corrections, shades of meaning and felicities of expression are now brought to view, enhancing greatly the clearness and beauty of the divinely-given records.

While improved scholarship has thus been enlarging acquaintance with the ancient tongues, our own English has not been fixed and immovable. No doubt the generally read version of the Scriptures has done much to prevent innovation, but a living, growing tongue experiences constant variation, and casts off from age to age once familiar words. To resist obstinately all recognition of these changes in a book intended to be in every hand, is to render certain portions obscure or unintelligible.

REASONS FOR A REVISION. — These are some of the reasons which have impressed upon Biblical scholars within the last generation the importance of a revision of the English Bible in common use. With all its confessed merits, the defects and errors were too glaring to be denied or overlooked. The conscience of the Christian church became more and more aroused. The duty of placing before the people a pure and unexceptionable text pressed more heavily. The assaults of gainsayers and enemies could not be successfully resisted. It was a painful thing for the teacher to be laboring to explain what, after all, was no part of the inspired volume, and for the preacher to find that the text upon which he had been discoursing was erroneously rendered. Neither was it a pleasant task to avoid misunderstandings, by encumbering a discourse with learned criticisms. Then the fact which could not be denied of the existence of thousands of various readings was magnified by assailants of the faith, and occasioned distrust and alarm in the heart of many an unlearned believer.

The battle with infidelity was fought at a disadvantage, while it was felt that there were useless weapons in the armory, and weak points in the walls of the citadel.

The conviction, therefore, has been of late years a growing one that a revision must come, and come ere very long. That it would be encountered by alarm and hostility was inevitable. This had been the fate of every attempt of this kind from the beginning. Jerome's great work, afterwards elevated by the Church of Rome to the rank of an infallible standard, awoke a furious tempest of opposition at the outset. But the necessity was now admitted by men not less known for their conservative opinions than for their scholarship.

ARCHBISHOP TRENCH ON REVISION.—Among the early prominent works indicating this conviction was that of Dr. Trench, now Archbishop of Dublin, in 1858, in which he says, " It is clear that the question, Are we, or are we not to have a new translation of the Scripture? or, rather, since few would propose this who do not wish to lift anchor, and loosen from its moorings the whole religious life of the English people, shall we, or shall we not have a new revision of the Authorized Version? is one which is presenting itself more and more familiarly to the minds of men." "Of the arguments against a revision none will deny the weight. Indeed, there are times when the whole matter presents itself as so full of difficulty and doubtful hazard, that one could be well content to resign all gains that would accrue from this revision, and only ask that things might remain as they are; but this, I am persuaded, is impossible. However we may be disposed to let the question alone, it will not let us alone. It has been too effectually stirred, ever again to go to sleep; and the difficulties with which it is surrounded, be they few or many, will have at no distant day to be encountered. The time will come when the perils of remaining where we are will be so manifestly greater than the perils of action, that action will become inevitable. There will be danger in both courses, for that saying of the Latin moralist is a profoundly true one, '*Nunquam periculum sine periculo vincitur;*' but the lesser danger will have to be chosen."

DIFFICULTIES OF REVISION.—But the importance and necessity of the work being admitted, the manner of proceeding was beset with great and obvious difficulties. The so-called Authorized Version was the common property and treasure of all who speak the English tongue. Its merits had commended it to almost universal acceptance. Although issuing from the Church of England, it was no less prized by the different bodies of non-conformists in that country, and by various Christian communions in our own land. It was a bond of union among those who differed materially from each other; a common standard of appeal. The wide diffusion of the Anglo-Saxon race had carried it over the world; and wherever one to whom the English language was vernacular found himself, he heard in public worship the same hallowed and venerated phrases and expressions. Some of the most eager advocates for revision trembled at the thought of losing so blessed a testimony to the unity of our faith, and felt that it would be a deplorable change to substitute several versions for the one that had obtained such supremacy and acceptance. The opinion was therefore strongly expressed by those who discussed the subject, that, in securing a more accurate book, the greatest care should be taken not to forfeit this happy unanimity.

This obstacle seemed at once to oppose the undertaking to supply this want by any one church. Jealousy and distrust would be inevitably awakened. The authority thus gained within the borders of the communion assuming this work would be met by prejudices awakened in other bodies. To bring delegates from all these communions together for consultation seemed an impracticable matter. If any Church should lead in the enterprise, the old historic Church which had produced the Authorized Version would seem evidently to be the one to take the initiative; and yet its ablest minds felt that the risk was very serious of failing to obtain general recognition, even if the Church of England could authoritatively sanction and adopt a revised version. Archbishop Trench remarks in the work above referred to, "With the exception of the Roman Catholics, the Authorized Version is common ground for all in England who call themselves Christians; is alike the heritage of all. But, even if English Dissenters acknowledge the necessity of a revision, which I conclude from many indications they do, it is idle to expect they would accept such at our hands. Two things then might happen: either they would adhere to the old version, which is not, indeed, very probable; or they would carry out a revision — it might be two or three — of their own. In either case the ground of a common Scripture, of an English Bible which they and we hold equally sacred, would be taken from us; the separation and division which are now the sorrow, and perplexity, and shame of England, would become more marked, more deeply fixed than ever."

It is evident that the difficulty which seemed so formidable to Dr. Trench would not be lighter in case of any other Christian body undertaking the work. This would be, in all probability, merely to provide a version of their own, and thus to cut themselves off, so far as this bond is concerned, from sympathy with fellow-believers.

Another difficulty suggests itself, in the way of proceeding by Church authority, and that is the danger of giving previous sanction to a work which, after all, might not prove acceptable. The safer way is evidently for a proposed version to be for a time before the public, subject to free examination, prior to its formal adoption.

And this seems to have been the history of the present English Bible. The title of "Authorized Version" conveys a not altogether correct impression. The work was undertaken by direction of the king, without any synodal action or consent, and when published seems to have been left to win its own way to acceptance and use. "The clause on the title-page 'appointed to be read in churches,' has, so far as is known, no authority, no edict of Convocation, no Act of Parliament, no decision of the Privy Council, no royal proclamation" (Eadie, Vol. II., p. 204). For some time after it was issued the Bishops' and the Geneva Bible were republished, extensively circulated, and the former held its old place in many churches. So that there is very little in the history of our present Bible to support the claim that a revision can only be undertaken and consummated by church authority.

At the same time it is evident that more is needed than individual enterprise or a self-constituted board of revisers. Men of high attainments and excellent judgment have made valuable contributions to a more faithful and exact presentation of the Divine Word, and eminent scholars have united to set forth different portions, but it is evident that none of these can obtain universal assent. The work that is eventually to take the place of the Bible of 1611 must not only engage the patient study of well-qualified minds, but it must come before the public with higher claims to attention than a self-constituted committee can command.

FIRST STEPS TOWARDS THE PRESENT REVISION.—These perplexities seem to have been happily solved in the present movement for revising the Authorized Version. It originated in the Convocation of the Province of Canterbury, an ecclesiastical body containing representatives from five-sixths of the Church of England. This assemblage of men of the highest position and most eminent character and scholarship in the Church which gave the present time-honored book, conferred the desirable sanction upon the revising body, without committing the church absolutely to their conclusions. It is no spontaneous, merely voluntary undertaking, in which the present revisers are combined, but one originating in an ecclesiastical Council of the greatest weight and respectability. May 6, 1870, resolutions were unanimously adopted by the upper house of the Convocation of Canterbury, and concurred in by a large majority of the lower house, to the following effect:

"1. That it is desirable that a revision of the Authorized Version of the Holy Scriptures be undertaken.

"2. That the revision be so conducted as to comprise both marginal renderings, and such emendations as it may be found necessary to insert in the text.

"3. That in the above resolutions we do not contemplate any new translation of the Bible, or any alteration of the language, except where, in the judgment of the most competent scholars, such change is necessary.

"4. That in such necessary changes, the style of the language employed in the existing version be closely followed.

"5. That it is desirable that Convocation should nominate a body of its own members to undertake the work of revision, who shall be at liberty to invite the co-operation of any eminent for scholarship, to whatever nation or religious body they may belong."

The language of clause 5 indicates the liberal and comprehensive spirit of the action that was adopted. The great work was not to be confined to members of the Anglican Church, but to be shared by representatives of the different bodies who have equal interest in the result. This principle was advocated strongly by Archbishop Trench, in the treatise above mentioned, and by Bishop Ellicott, in the introduction to his work on the Revision of the New Testament, and was fully admitted by the Convocation.

AMERICAN CO-OPERATION.—In accordance with this action, the committee appointed, consisting of eight members of each house of Convocation, proceeded to invite eminent scholars and divines, as well from different bodies of non-conformists as from the Church of England, to join in this work. Among these are found names the most distinguished for biblical and classical scholarship. The insertion of the significant word "nation" in the action above recited, showed the desire for participation in the proposed work beyond the bounds of the British Empire, as well as beyond the limits of the established Church.

Measures were accordingly taken to obtain the co-operation of American scholars, in the hope of making the new version, like the old one, a bond of union between two great nations speaking the same language. Twenty-five persons, representing the principal Protestant communions in the United States, were invited to act in co-operation with the English revisers, and have been holding regular monthly sessions for the last seven years. There has been constant and confidential interchange of results between the committees on each side of the Atlantic, and the joint work has been going forward in a harmonious and satisfactory manner.

The final acceptance of the result is to be hereafter shown. The revisers do not ask or expect an immediate and inconsiderate approval. They will submit their conclusions to the calm and mature examination of the great Christian public, to be judged upon their own merits. It is confidently suggested to candid men who love God's word, and desire it to be presented in the greatest attainable purity, that probably no method of procedure could have been devised for securing that object, less open to objection, and combining greater advantage and promise, than that which has been adopted.

GENERAL INDEX.

Abbot, Ezra, 12, 86.
Acts, MSS. of, 95, 96.
Adams, W., 13.
Addison on A. V., 37.
Æschylus, MSS. of, 95.
Aiken, C. A., 11, 151.
Alexander, W. L., 7.
Alexandrian MS., 74, 95.
Alford, Dean, 10.
American language, 117.
American Revision Committee, 11, 14, 15, 179.
Ancient translations: see VERSIONS.
Anderson, T. D., 13.
ANGLO-AMERICAN BIBLE REVISION, 10, 14.
Angus, J., 9.
Antiquities of the Holy Land, 62.
Antwerp Polyglot, 74, 158.
Aorist, errors in the use of the, 106, 107, 126, 128.
Aquila, version of, 44, 74.
Arabic language, 61, 76.
—— MSS., 96.
—— versions, 62, 75, 96.
ARCHAISMS, OR OBSOLETE AND UNUSUAL WORDS OR PHRASES IN THE ENGLISH BIBLE, 144.
Armenian MSS., 96.
Article, definite, 68, 101.
Assyria, antiquities in, 62.
Authorized Version:
—— a classic, 37–42.
—— accuracy of, 56.
—— associations of, 41.
—— authority of, 48.

Authorized Version, authors of, 31, 39, 99.
—— beauties of, 34, 41.
—— character of, 39.
—— conservative influence of, 40.
—— critical apparatus of, 46, 73–79, 172.
—— defects of, 47, 62.
—— errors of, 64, 80–85, 99–112, 129–144.
—— estimation of, 16, 34, 113, 172.
—— eulogies on, 16, 34, 37, 39, 40, 113, 172.
—— excellencies of, 171.
—— Faber on, 42.
—— Greek text of, 17, 93, 113, 118–125.
—— helps for translating, 72–79.
—— history of, 14, 15, 20, 30–37, 39, 44, 60, 61, 70, 72–79, 99, 177.
—— inaccuracies of, 68, 80–85, 99–112.
—— infelicities of, 111, 137.
—— instructions regarding, 31.
—— italics in, 157–165.
—— obscurities of, 138.
—— obsolete words in, 145.
—— preface of, 50.
—— proper names of, 151–156.
—— standard of English, 35, 37, 44.
—— style of, 35, 38, 39, 45, 47, 52, 119, 140, 171.
—— translators of, 31, 39.
—— verbal differences and agreements in, 133–143.
—— Wycliffe and, 30.

Babylonia, schools in, 54.
Bacon, style of, 38.

Barnes, A. S., 13.
Bath and Wells, Bishop of, 7.
Bengel, labors of, 97.
Bensly, Robert L., 7.
Beza, version of, 28, 93, 94, 158.
Bible, a classic, 37-42.
—— Bishops', 29, 34, 39, 40, 158.
—— Chapters of, 17, 166.
—— Coverdale's, 25, 26, 28, 32, 39, 158.
—— Cranmer's, 29, 32, 39.
—— divisions of, 166-169.
—— Great, 26, 158.
—— Matthew's, 26, 28, 32, 39.
—— Paragraphs of, 166.
—— Taverner's, 27.
—— Translations of: see VERSIONS.
—— Verses of, 28, 166.
—— Versions of: see VERSIONS.
—— Whitchurch's, 32.
Biblical science, advances in, 49, 60, 99, 172.
Biblical style, 45.
Bickersteth, Dean, 9.
Birrell, John, 7.
Bishop, N., 13.
Bishops' Bible, 29, 34, 39, 40, 158.
Blakesley, Dean, 9.
Bomberg, Bible of, 53.
Bottcher, Hebrew Grammar of, 76.
Britain, Christianity in, 22.
British Museum, 74.
Brown, David, 9.
Brown, J. M., 13.
Browne, Bishop E. H., 7.
Burr, J. K., 12.
Buxtorf, John, Hebrew works of, 61, 62, 75.
Buxtorf, John, Jr., labors of, 61.

Cambridge MS., 95.
—— University Press, 19.
Campbell, George, version of, 41.
Canterbury, Canon of, 7.
—— convocation of, 14, 178.
—— Dean of, 7.
—— revision, 178.

Capellus, labors of, 57.
Castellus, labors of, 61, 76.
Catholic Epistles, 95.
Cauldwell, W. A., 13.
Chaldee paraphrases, 75.
—— targums, 62.
—— versions, 57, 75.
Chambers, Talbot W., 11, 37.
Chance, Frank, 7.
Change, given to, 81.
Chapters of the Bible, 17, 166.
—— headings of, 17.
Chase, Thomas, 12, 157.
Chayim, Jacob ben, 54.
Chenery, Thomas, 7.
Cheyne, T. K., 7.
Christianity in Britain, 22.
Church of Rome and the Scriptures, 29, 174.
Classical authors, text of, 86, 95.
Clermont MS., 93.
Codex Amiatinus, 75.
Codex Bezæ, 95
Coins of the Bible, 118.
Coleridge on A. V., 37.
Complutensian Polyglot, 74, 93, 94.
Conant, T. J., labors of, 11, 82.
CONSERVATISM IN RESPECT TO CHANGES IN THE ENGLISH AND THE GREEK TEXT, 113.
Convocation of Canterbury, 14.
Cook, Canon, 10.
Coptic MS., 96.
Copyists, errors of, 97.
—— rules of, 55.
Corn-fields, 117.
Coverdale, version of, 25, 26, 28, 32, 39, 158.
Cranmer's Bible, 29, 32, 39.
Critical Apparatus for A. A. Version, 46, 94-97.
Criticism, advances in, 49, 99, 172.
—— of Old Testament, 54.
Crooks, G. R., 12.
Crosby, Howard, 12, 144.
Curetonian MS., 96.

GENERAL INDEX. 183

CURRENT VERSION OF THE SCRIPTURES AS COMPARED WITH OUR PRESENT NEEDS, 48.
Cursive MSS., 96.

Davidson, A. B., 7.
Davidson, D. S., 56.
Davies, Professor, 8.
Day, George E., 11, 72.
De Dieu, labors of, 76.
De Rossi, labors of, 57, 62.
De Witt, J., 11.
Devil, name of, 142.
Diodati, version of, 77, 158.
Divisions of the Bible, 166–169.
Dodge, William E., 13.
Douglas, George, 7.
Driver, S. R., 7.
Dutch versions, 25, 37.
Duty of Revisionists, 70.
Dwight, Timothy, 12, 113.
Dyer, H., 13.

Eadie, John, 10.
Egypt, antiquities of, 62.
—— MSS. of, 96.
—— river of, 63.
Ellicott, Bishop, 9.
Elliot, J., 13.
Elliott, C. J., 7.
Elizabeth, style of her time, 38.
ENGLISH BIBLE AS A CLASSIC, 37.
English language and the A. V., 34, 36, 38, 115, 127, 143, 144–150, 160, 171.
English Revision Company, 7, 14, 15.
Ephraem MS., 95.
Epistle to the Hebrews, 110, 139.
Erasmus, New Testament of, 93.
Errors in geography, 62, 79.
—— Greek article, 101.
—— Hebrew Grammar, 67.
—— prepositions and particles, 103.
—— proper names, 64.
—— verbs, 105.
Ethiopic language, 61.

Ethiopic version, 75.
Ewald, Hebrew Grammar of, 76.
—— labors of, 61.

Faber, F. W., on A. V., 42.
Fairbairn, P., 8.
Fancher, E. L., 13.
Field, Frederick, 8.
Frankel, labors of, 57.
French versions, 77.
Fronsdorf, labors of, 57.
Fuerst, labors of, 61, 83.

Geden, J. D., 8.
Geneva Bible, 28, 29, 30, 32, 39, 41, 93.
Geography of the Bible, 62, 79.
German language, 127.
—— versions, 25, 77.
Gesenius, Hebrew Grammar of, 76.
—— labors of, 61, 83.
Ginsburg, C. D., 8, 57.
Gospels, MSS. of, 95, 96.
Gotch, F. W., 8.
Gothic MSS., 96.
Grain-fields, 117.
Great Bible, 26, 158.
Greek article, errors in, 101.
—— authors, 86, 93, 94, 95, 127.
—— criticism, 16.
—— imperatives, 131.
—— imperfect, 129.
—— language, 25, 35, 47, 50, 127, 152, 154, 157, 172.
—— manuscripts, 17, 45, 49, 54, 86, 93–98.
—— middle voice, 132.
—— non-indicative, 131.
—— perfect, 130.
—— tenses, 127.
—— Testaments, 28, 93, 94.
—— text of A. A. V., 46, 94, 118.
—— text of A. V., 45, 86, 93.
—— verb, 126.
—— versions, 44.
GREEK VERB IN THE NEW TESTAMENT, 126–132.

Green, W. Henry, 11, 60.
—— Hebrew Grammar of, 76.
Griesbach, labors of, 97, 98.

Hackett, Horatio B., 12.
Hadley, James, 12.
Hallam on the A. V., 37.
Hare, Augustus, on the A. V., 40.
Hare, G. Emlen, 11, 48.
Harrison, Archdeacon, 7.
Havemeyer, J. C., 13.
Hebrew criticism, advances in, 16.
—— Grammars, 75.
—— language, 22, 25, 35, 47, 50, 55, 67, 70, 72, 73, 75, 76, 78, 152, 154, 157, 160.
—— manuscripts, 54, 57.
—— philology of the A. V., 61.
—— professors of, 15.
—— restorations of, 57.
—— text, 17, 53, 54, 57.
—— vowels, 62.
HEBREW PHILOLOGY AND BIBLICAL SCIENCE, 60–71.
Hebrew Text of the Old Testament, 53–59.
Hebrews, Epistle to the, 110, 139.
HELPS FOR TRANSLATING THE HEBREW SCRIPTURES AT THE TIME THE AUTHORIZED VERSION WAS MADE, 72–79.
Henry VIII. and the Bible, 25, 27.
Henry, Matthew, 81.
Hervey, Bishop, A. C., 7.
Hippopotamus of Job, 82.
Hodge, Charles, 12.
Homer, text of, 86.
Homœoteleuton, 88.
Hort, F. J. A., labors of, 9, 98.
Houbigant, labors of, 57, 62.
Humphry, W. G., 9.
Huxley, T. H., on A. V., 37.

INACCURACIES OF THE AUTHORIZED VERSION OF THE OLD TESTAMENT, 80–85.
INACCURACIES OF THE AUTHORIZED VERSION IN RESPECT OF GRAMMAR AND EXEGESIS, 99–112.
Inaccuracy in the construction, 68.
Italian versions, 77, 158.
Italics in the Bible, 17, 18, 157–165.
ITALICS IN THE ENGLISH BIBLE, 157–165.
Italics, errors caused by, 162.
—— felicitous use of, 163.
—— origin of, 157.
—— revision of the, 164.
—— superfluous use of, 159.

James I., style of time of, 38.
—— version of: see AUTHORIZED VERSION.
Jebb, Canon, 8.
Jerome, versions of, 52, 55, 74, 158, 174.
Jerusalem, Syriac MS. of, 96.
Jessup, M. K., 13.
Jews, criticism of, 57.
—— persecution of, 55.
—— schools of, 54.
Job, day of his birth, 81.
—— English version of, 81.
—— Hippopotamus of, 82.
—— War horse of, 82.
John, style of, 140.
Josephus on Old Testament text, 55.
Juda, Leo, 25.
Junius, version of, 158.

Kay, W., 8.
Kendrick, A. C., 12, 99.
Kennedy, Canon, 9.
Kennicott, labors of, 57, 62.
Kilbye, Dr. R., 81.
King James's version: see AUTHORIZED VERSION.
Krauth, Charles P., 11, 22.

Lachman, labors of, 97, 98.
Language, American, 117.
—— Arabic, 61, 76.
—— English, 34, 36, 38, 115, 127, 143, 144–150, 160, 171.

Language, Ethiopic, 61.
—— German, 127.
—— of the A. V., 17.
—— Syriac, 61, 76.
Languages, changes in, 44, 49, 134, 173.
—— Semitic, 73, 76.
Latin authors, 93.
—— manuscripts, 96.
—— versions, 22, 25, 26, 27, 77, 174.
Leathes, Stanley, 8.
Lectionaries, MSS. of, 96.
Lee, Archdeacon, 9.
—— Bishop, 12, 170.
Lewis, Tayler, 11.
Lightfoot, Bishop, labors of, 9, 98.
—— on the A. V., 47.
Llandaff, Bishop of, 7.
London Polyglot of 1657, 62.
Lord's Prayer, 89.
Lowth, Bishop, labors of, 41, 57.
Lumby, John R., 8.
Luther, version of, 23, 24, 25, 77.

Macaulay, Lord, on A. V., 37.
MacGill, Professor, 8.
Maidstone, Archdeacon of, 7.
Manuscripts:
—— Alexandrian, 74, 95.
—— Arabic, 96.
—— Armenian, 96.
—— Cambridge, 95.
—— Clermont, 93.
—— Coptic, 96.
—— Curetonian, 96.
—— Cursive, 96.
—— Egyptian, 96.
—— Ephraem, 95.
—— Gothic, 96.
—— Greek, 17, 45, 49, 54, 86, 93-98.
—— Hebrew, 54, 57.
—— Jerusalem, 96.
—— Lectionaries, 96.
—— Memphitic, 96.
—— Sahidic, 96.
—— Sinaitic, 54, 74, 95.

Manuscripts:
—— Slavonic, 96.
—— Syriac, 96.
—— Thebaic, 96.
—— Uncial, 17, 95.
—— Vatican, 54, 95.
Marginal readings, 54.
Mark, style of, 140.
Marsh, George P., 38.
Masoretic text, 17, 54, 62, 73, 167.
Masorites, 54.
Matthew, Thomas, Bible of, 26, 32, 39.
Mead, Charles M., 11.
Memphitic MS., 96.
Merivale, Dean, 10.
Metrical arrangement, 18.
Mill, labors of, 97.
Milligan, William, 10.
Moberly, Bishop, 9.
Montanus, Arias, 157.
Moulton, W. F., 10.
Münster, S., version of, 26, 157.

Names, proper, changes in, 151.
—— harmonizing of, 155.
—— inconsistencies in, 152.
—— of the Bible, 151-156.
Nebuchadnezzar, dream of, 82.
New Testament:
—— manuscripts of, 17, 45, 49, 54, 86, 93-98.
—— Rheims, 29.
—— text of, 17, 57, 86-98.
—— various readings of, 56, 91.
NEW TESTAMENT TEXT, 86-98.
Newman, Francis W., on A. V., 37.
Newman, John H., 10.
—— on A. V., 37.
Newth, S., 10.
Nile River, 63.
Norton, Andrews, on A. V., 91.

Obsolete significations, 145.
—— words, 149.
Old Testament text, 55, 56, 57.
—— various readings of, 56.

OLDER ENGLISH AND THE AUTHORIZED VERSIONS, 22–36.
Ollivant, Bishop A., 7.
Origen, labors of, 44, 74, 157, 158.
—— polyglot of, 44.
Osgood, Howard, 11, 53.
Oxford University Press, 19.

Packard, Joseph, 11, 80.
Pages, headings of, 17, 18.
Pagninus, version of, 158.
Palestina, 63.
Palmer, Edwin, 10.
Paper, invention of, 23.
Paragraphs, 17.
PARAGRAPHS, CHAPTERS, AND VERSES OF THE BIBLE, 166–169.
Parallelism, 79, 167.
Paris, Polyglot of 1645, 62, 75.
Parker, Archbishop, 29.
Participle aorist, 107.
Particles, errors of, in A. V., 104.
Paul, style of, 141.
Pauline Epistles, 93, 95, 96.
Pentateuch, Samaritan, 75.
Perowne, Dean, 8.
Persian version, 75.
Peshito version, 44, 96.
Philodemus, fragments of, 95.
Philology, advances in, 60, 76.
—— Hebrew, 60–71.
Philoxenian, Syriac MS., 96.
Pinsker, labors of, 57.
Plato, text of, 86.
Plumptre, Edward H., 8.
Pococke, labors of, 76.
Poetical books of Old Testament, 79, 167, 169.
Polyglot Bibles:
—— Antwerp, 74, 158.
—— Complutensian, 93, 94.
—— London, 1657, 62.
—— Origen's, 44.
—— Paris, 1645, 62, 75.
Potter, Henry C., 13.
Potter, Howard, 13.

Prepositions, errors of in A. V., 103.
Printing, invention of, 23.
PROPER NAMES OF THE BIBLE, 151–156.
Prose of the Bible, arrangement of, 18.
Provincialisms, 118.
Psalms, Jerome's version of, 74.
Publication of A. A. Version, 19, 20.
Punctuation of the Bible, 17.
Puritans and the Bible, 30.
Pusey, Edward B., 10.

Rabbinical Commentaries, 53, 61, 62, 76, 78.
Raleigh, style of, 38.
Readings, various, 46, 56, 86, 93, 124.
REASONS FOR A NEW REVISION OF THE SCRIPTURES IN ENGLISH, 43–47.
Renderings, erroneous: see AUTHORIZED VERSION.
Restorations of Hebrew, 57.
Revelation, MSS. of, 96.
Revision, Anglo-American:
—— auspices of, 20, 21, 41, 70, 72, 73, 94, 172.
—— demand for, 43.
—— difficulties of, 175.
—— materials for, 46, 94–98.
—— objections to, 170.
—— origin of, 14, 178.
—— principles of, 16, 41.
—— progress of, 19.
—— prospects of, 21, 97.
—— publication of, 19, 20.
—— reasons for, 43–47, 170–180.
—— Trench on, 174.
"Revision of the Hebrew Text," by Davidson, 56.
REVISION OF THE SCRIPTURES, 170–180.
REVISION OF THE SCRIPTURES IN ENGLISH, 43–47.
Revisionists, duty of the, 70.
Reynolds, John, labors of, 33, 72.
—— suggests the A. V., 30.
Rheims, New Testament of, 29.
Riddle, Matthew B., 12, 126.

Roberts, Alexander, 10.
Rogers, John, version of, 26, 28, 32, 39.
Rose, Henry John, 8.
Roye assists Tyndale, (?) 24.
Ruskin, John, on A. V., 37.

Sahidic manuscript, 96.
Samaria, woe to, 84.
Samaritan version, 75.
Saxon version, 22.
Sayce, A. H., 8.
Schaff, Philip, 11, 12, 14.
Schultens, Albert, labors of, 61, 76.
Scott, Dean, 9.
Scrivener, Fred. H. A., 10, 98.
Selden, John, Table Talk of, 77.
Selwyn, William, 8.
Semitic languages, 73, 76.
Septuagint, 44, 57, 58, 74, 75, 157.
Shakspeare, style of, 38.
Shepard, Elliott F., 13.
Short, Charles, 12.
Sinaitic manuscript, 54, 74, 95.
Slavonic manuscript, 96.
Smith, George V., 10.
Smith, Henry B., 12.
Smith, Robert P., 7.
Smith, Roswell, 13.
Smith, Wm. R., 8.
Solomon, horses of, 83.
Sophocles, manuscripts of, 95.
Spanish versions, 77, 158.
Spelling, changes in, 144, 149.
Stanley, Dean, 9.
Stephens, Robert, Greek Testaments of, 28, 93, 94.
Storrs, Richard S., 13.
Stowe, Calvin E., 11.
Strack, labors of, 57.
Strong, James, 11, 166.
Style, Hare on, 40.
Swift on A. V., 37.
Symmachus, version of, 44, 74.
Syriac language, 61, 76.
—— manuscripts, 96.
—— version, 44, 62, 75, 76.

Talmud, collection of, 54.
—— criticism of, 57, 58.
Talmudists, rules of, 54, 55.
Targums and A. V., 75.
Taverner, Bible of, 27.
Taylor, Andrew L., 13.
Tenses, Greek, 127.
—— of A. V., 105.
Thayer, J. Henry, 12, 133.
Thebaic manuscript, 96.
Theodotion, version of, 44, 74.
Thirlwall, Bishop, 8.
Thomas of Harkel, revision of, 96.
Three Heavenly Witnesses, 89.
Thucydides, text of, 86.
Tischendorf, labors of, 74, 97, 98.
Tracy, Charles, 13.
Translations: see VERSIONS.
Translator, duty of, 58.
Tregelles, S. P., labors of, 10, 97, 98.
Tremellius, version of, 158.
Trench, Archbishop, 9, 174–177.
Trevor, John B., 13.
Trinity, doctrine of, 92.
Troutbeck, J., 10.
TRUE CONSERVATISM IN RESPECT TO CHANGES IN THE ENGLISH AND THE GREEK TEXT, 113–125.
Tyndale's version, 24, 25, 27, 28, 30, 32, 39.

Uncial manuscripts, 17, 95.
University Presses, 19.
UNWARRANTABLE VERBAL DIFFERENCES AND AGREEMENTS IN THE ENGLISH VERSION, 133–143.

Valera, Cypriano de, version of, 158.
Van Dyck, C. V. A., 11.
Vatican manuscript, 54, 95.
Vaughan, Charles J., 10.
Verbs, errors in, 105.
Verses of the Bible, 28, 166.
Versions of the Bible or of parts thereof:
—— Ancient, 73.

Versions of the Bible or of parts thereof:
—— Anglo-American, 46, 52, 94–98.
—— Aquila, 44, 74.
—— Arabic, 62, 75, 96.
—— Authorized: see AUTHORIZED VERSION.
—— Bezæ, 28, 93, 94, 158.
—— Bomberg, 53.
—— Campbell, 41.
—— Chaldee, 57, 58, 62, 75.
—— Conant, 82.
—— Coverdale, 25, 26, 28, 32, 39, 158.
—— Cranmer, 29, 32, 39.
—— Diodati, 77, 158.
—— Dutch, 25, 37.
—— Ethiopic, 75.
—— French, 77.
—— German, 25, 77.
—— Greek, 44.
—— Italian, 77, 158.
—— Jerome, 52, 55, 74, 158.
—— Junius, 158.
—— Latin, 22, 25, 26, 27, 77, 174.
—— Lowth, 41.
—— Luther, 23, 24, 25, 77.
—— Münster, S., 26, 157.
—— Pagninus, 158.
—— Persian, 75.
—— Peshito, 44, 96.
—— Rheims, 29.
—— Rogers, John, 26, 28, 29, 32.
—— Samaritan, 75.
—— Saxon, 22.
—— Spanish, 77, 158.

Versions of the Bible or of parts thereof:
—— Symmachus, 44, 74.
—— Syriac, 44, 62, 75, 76.
—— Theodotion, 44, 74.
—— Tremellius, 158.
—— Tyndale, 24, 25, 27, 28, 30, 32, 39.
—— Valera, Cypriano de, 158.
—— Various, 22, 24–36, 40, 44, 73, 77, 96, 157, 158.
—— Vulgate, 22, 27, 52, 55, 74, 75, 77, 94, 96, 158, 174.
—— Whittingham, 28.
—— Wycliffe, 22, 30, 38.
Vowels, Hebrew, 62.

War horse of Job, 82.
Warren, S. D., 13.
Warren, W. F., 12.
Washburn, E. A., 12.
Weir, Professor, 8.
Westcott, Brooke F., labors of, 10, 98.
Wetstein, labors of, 97, 98.
Whitchurch, Bible of, 32.
White, Norman, 13.
Whittingham, version of, 28.
Wilberforce, Bishop, 10.
Winchester, Bishop of, 7.
Winston, F. S., 13.
Woman taken in adultery, 90, 124.
Woolsey, Theodore D., 12, 43.
Wordsworth, Bishop, 8, 9.
Wright, William, 8.
Wright, William Aldis, 8.
Wycliffe, version of, 22, 30, 38.

INDEX TO TEXTS CITED.

	PAGE
Genesis 1, generally,	167
—— 1 : 10	83
—— 2 : 1-3	167
—— 2 : 4	167
—— 4 : 23, 24	167
—— 5, generally	153
—— 10 : 15, 19	153
—— 12 : 6	65
—— 12 : 9	63
—— 12 : 16	148
—— 15 : 6	142
—— 17 : 7	50
—— 22 : 15, 17, 18	51
—— 25 : 4	153
—— 28 : 12	147
—— 36 : 24	67
—— 37, generally	154
—— 37 : 3	66
—— 39, generally	154
—— 46 : 13	153
Exodus 2 : 11, 12	51
—— 9 : 31	149
—— 11 : 2	66
—— 28 : 11	145
—— 29 : 36, 40	147
—— 30 : 13	110
—— 30 : 25, 35	146
—— 34 : 13	65
—— 36 : 13, 38	145
—— 37 : 29	146
—— 38 : 24	150
Leviticus 16 : 8	65
Numbers 5 : 13	150
—— 7 : 13	147
—— 21 : 14	64
—— 23 : 22	67
—— 23 : 23	69
—— 24 : 4	70
—— 24 : 17	64

	PAGE
Numb. 26, generally	154
—— 26 : 23	153
—— 32 : 17	147
—— 34 : 5	63
Deuteronomy 2 : 23	152
—— 4 : 2	60
—— 12 : 32	60
—— 21 : 4	63
—— 28 : 27	147
—— 33 : 6	160
Joshua 9 : 5	145
—— 11 : 16	63
—— 17 : 1	70
—— 24 : 33	63
Judges 5 : 2	65
—— 9 : 46	148
—— 9 : 53	146
—— 12, generally	154
—— 12 : 14	147
—— 15 : 8	66
—— 15 : 19	64
—— 16 . 11	150
—— 18 : 7	149
—— 20 : 26	64
—— 21 : 19	68
Ruth 3 : 15	66
I. Samuel 1 : 1	64
—— 2 : 3	160
—— 9 : 5	150
—— 17 : 22	149
—— 20 : 40	149
—— 22 : 4	148
—— 27 : 10	150
II. Samuel 1 : 18	64
—— 8 : 1	64
—— 18 : 23	150

	PAGE
I. Kings 4 : 24	152
—— 10 : 28	83
II. Kings 4 : 35	149
—— 16 : 10	153
—— 22 : 14	65
I. Chronicles	
—— 1, generally	153
—— 1 : 1	153
—— 1 : 33	153
—— 2, generally	154
—— 3 : 10	153
—— 7 : 1	153
—— 29 : 11	89
II. Chronicles	
—— 4 : 12	147
—— 9 : 14	145
—— 12 : 16	153
—— 21 : 20	150
Ezra 9 : 3	145
—— 9 : 12	150
Nehemiah 13 : 26	147
Esther 10 : 3	150
Job 3 : 3	81
—— 3 : 11	160
—— 9 : 33	145
—— 18 : 19	147
—— 26 : 13	65
—— 30 : 20, 25	160
—— 39, generally	82
—— 39 : 4	150
—— 39 : 24	82
—— 39 : 40	82
—— 40, generally	82
—— 40 : 19, 23	82
—— 41 : 18	149

	PAGE		PAGE		PAGE
Psalms 3 : 4, 5	67	Isaiah 16 : 13	65	Habakkuk 2 : 6, 16	65
— 4 : 1	68	— 18 : 2	63	— 3 : 3	67
— 7 : 13	69	— 19 : 10	66		
— 10 : 4	69	— 27 : 1	65	Zechariah 1 : 21	148
— 19 : 3	69, 162	— 28 : 1, 3, 4	84	— 7 : 12	146
— 22 : 30	69	— 28 : 15-19	83		
— 35 : 15, 21	146	— 28 : 17	84	Malachi 3 : 1	51
— 37 : 40	67	— 28 : 20	83, 84		
— 40 : 11	67	— 38 : 14	148	Matthew 1 : 25	90, 129
— 47 : 8	68	— 38 : 18	160	— 2 : 2	129
— 48 : 1	68	— 40 : 12	148	— 2 : 22	104, 130
— 59 : 17	68, 69	— 47 : 8	149	— 3 : 4	118
— 59 : 19	69			— 3 : 5, 6	130
— 66 : 12	150	Jeremiah 1 : 15	83	— 3 : 15	161
— 71 : 22	65	— 8 : 7	147	— 4 : 6	104
— 73 : 16	150	— 10 : 22	149	— 4 : 25	118
— 75 : 5	160	— 17 : 1	146	— 5 : 10	138
— 91 : 5, 6	160	— 24 : 2	150	— 5 : 12	131
— 96 : 12, 13	168	— 25 : 20	152	— 5 : 16, 17	131
— 98 : 8, 9	168	— 38 : 11	145	— 5 : 22	136
— 109 : 4	163	— 39 : 3	64	— 5 : 44	88
— 124 : 3	147	— 49 : 31	150	— 5 : 45	132
		— 50 : 36	148	— 5 : 48	131
Proverbs 8 : 12	150			— 6 : 1	131
— 8 : 23	145	Ezekiel 3 : 9	146	— 6 : 2, 3	131
— 8 : 27	150	— 13 : 10, 18, 20	66	— 6 : 10	140
— 24 : 21	81	— 23 : 15	66	— 6 : 12	121
		— 27 : 9, 16, 19, 21,		— 6 : 13	89, 124
Eccles. 10 : 1	146	22	150	— 6 : 25	150
— 12 : 13	163	— 27 : 11, 17	64	— 8 : 24	105
		— 29 : 10	63	— 9 : 2	105
Song of Solomon		— 30 : 6	63	— 9 : 13	88
— 1 : 14	147	— 34 : 31	69	— 9 : 24	129
— 2 : 12	147			— 10 : 22	142
— 4 : 13	147	Daniel 2 : 5	82	— 10 : 23	121
— 7 : 5	65	— 2 : 9	83	— 12 : 5, 7	135
		— 3 : 21	145	— 14 : 8	147
Isaiah 3 : 18	147	— 3 : 28	83	— 15 : 36	130
— 3 : 20	66	— 7 : 9	83	— 16 : 2, 3	89
— 6 : 13	84			— 16 : 14	161
— 7 : 16	68	Hosea 3 : 1	65	— 17 : 21	89
— 8 : 2	153	— 4 : 18	65	— 17 : 24	109
— 8 : 19	148	— 11 : 12	65	— 18 : 11	89
— 8 : 21	145			— 18 : 24, 28	149
— 9 : 1	65	Joel 2 : 24	144	— 19 : 8	106
— 10 : 14	148	— 3 : 4	63	— 20 : 16	89
— 10 : 28	149			— 20 : 23	162
— 13 : 3	68	Obadiah 12-14	67	— 21 : 44	89
— 13 : 21	67			— 22 : 14	89
— 13 : 22	67	Nahum 2 : 3	66	— 23 : 6	150
— 14 : 22	147	— 2 : 7	64, 145	— 23 : 14	89
— 14 : 29, 31	63	— 2 : 12	145	— 23 : 35	136
— 15 : 2	64	— 3 : 8	64	— 23 : 44	136
— 15 : 5	64	— 3 : 19	149	— 24 : 12	103

INDEX TO TEXTS CITED. 191

Reference	PAGE
Matthew 21 : 21	106
—— 24 : 30	104
—— 25 : 7	150
—— 25 : 14	162
—— 25 : 28	105
—— 25 : 32	135
—— 25 : 46	141
—— 26 : 49	105
—— 27 : 35	89
Mark 1 : 2	90
—— 1 : 27	121
—— 2 : 17	88
—— 4 : 37	105
—— 5 : 34	142
—— 6 : 11	89
—— 6 : 22	49
—— 6 : 25	149
—— 6 : 41	130
—— 7 : 16	89
—— 8 : 6	130
—— 9 : 22	121
—— 9 : 23	90, 121
—— 9 : 44, 46	89
—— 10 : 52	142
—— 11 : 26	89
—— 12 : 38	139
—— 13 : 21	149
—— 13 : 34	162
—— 15 : 28	89
—— 16 : 9-20	89, 124
Luke 1 : 59	106
—— 2 : 7, 14	90
—— 3 : 15	161
—— 4 : 6	105
—— 4 : 44	90
—— 5 : 3, 7	130
—— 5 : 32	88
—— 6 : 1	90
—— 6 : 27, 28	88
—— 7 : 4	150
—— 7 : 5	101
—— 7 : 38	105
—— 7 : 41	149
—— 7 : 42	150
—— 7 : 50	142
—— 8 : 48	124, 142
—— 9 : 16	130
—— 9 : 55, 56	89, 90
—— 10 : 41	116
—— 11 : 2	140
—— 11 : 19	90
—— 12 : 58	144, 161
Luke 14 : 5	90
—— 14 : 10	150
—— 15 : 17, 22	121
—— 16 : 5	160
—— 17 : 7	149
—— 17 : 36	89
—— 18 : 42	142
—— 19 : 13	150
—— 19 : 16, 17	90
—— 20 : 46	139
—— 21 : 9	149
—— 21 : 19	109
—— 22 : 43, 44	89
—— 23 : 15	90, 122
—— 23 : 17	89
—— 23 : 34	89, 90
—— 23 : 44	136
—— 23 : 46	108
—— 24 : 12	89, 161
—— 24 : 25	136
—— 24 : 40	89
—— 24 : 51	90
John 1 : 3	106
—— 1 : 4	103
—— 1 : 5	148
—— 1 : 14	109
—— 1 : 18	90
—— 1 : 21, 25	103
—— 3 : 10	101
—— 3 : 13	90
—— 3 : 34	162
—— 4 : 27	102
—— 4 : 38	106
—— 5 : 3, 4	89, 124
—— 5 : 35	102
—— 6 : 39	131
—— 7 : 8	90
—— 7 : 53 to 8 : 11	89, 90, 124
—— 8 : 6	161
—— 8 : 46	150
—— 8 : 58	136
—— 10 : 4, 14	122
—— 11 : 3, 5	134
—— 13 : 7	134
—— 13 : 10	135
—— 14 : 1	131
—— 14 : 14	90
—— 15 : 26	163
—— 20 : 5, 11	160
—— 21 : 17	134
—— 21 : 25	89
Acts 2 : 47	142
Acts 5 : 30	109
—— 7 : 42	161
—— 7 : 45	156
—— 7 : 59	163
—— 8 : 37	89
—— 9 : 5, 6	89, 94
—— 10 : 3	148
—— 10 : 29	161
—— 11 : 20	90
—— 13 : 18	89
—— 15 : 34	89
—— 16 : 7	90
—— 18 : 5	122
—— 19 : 2	109
—— 19 : 15	134
—— 20 : 28	90
—— 20 : 37	105
—— 21 : 3	108
—— 21 : 5, 6, 7	108
—— 21 : 15	116, 149
—— 22 : 10	89
—— 23 : 1	162
—— 23 : 9	122
—— 23 : 22	161
—— 24 : 6-8	89
—— 24 : 25	116
—— 26 : 14	89
—— 26 : 24	141
—— 26 : 28	141
—— 27 : 12	154
—— 27 : 40	144
—— 28 : 8, 13	149
—— 28 : 29	89
Romans, generally	138
—— 1 : 17	102
—— 3 : 21	102, 106
—— 4, generally	143
—— 4 : 3	143
—— 4 : 17	163
—— 4 : 19	50
—— 5 : 4	116
—— 5 : 5	106
—— 5 : 6, 8	107
—— 5 : 11	138, 147
—— 5 : 12	107, 129
—— 5 : 17, 19	107
—— 6 : 2, 4	107
—— 7 : 4	107
—— 7 : 6	94
—— 7 : 7, 8	136
—— 7 : 25	105
—— 9 : 22	143
—— 9 : 29	155

	PAGE		PAGE		PAGE
Romans 11 : 4	161	Galatians 5 : 1	123	Hebrews 9 : 1	105
— 11 : 6	89	— 5 : 20, 23	116	— 9 : 12	162
— 12 : 1	116			— 10 : 38	162, 164
— 12 : 17	148	Ephesians, generally	138	— 11 : 10	102
— 14 : 10	90			— 11 : 17	105
— 14 : 23	148	— 3 : 9	90	— 11 : 23	150
— 16 : 24	89	— 4 : 1	148	— 12 : 7	123
		— 4 : 14	161		
I. Corinthians		— 5 : 21	91	James 2 : 2, 3	135
— 1 : 18	142			— 2 : 9	150
— 1 : 19	116	Philippians 3 : 14	149	— 5 : 1	149
— 2 : 11	134	— 4 : 6	116, 149		
— 4 : 4	48			I. Peter 1 : 22	162
— 6 : 20	122	Colossians, generally	138	— 3 : 11	148
— 7 : 31	141			— 3 : 14	138
— 9 : 24	149	— 1 : 27	91	— 3 : 15	91
— 9 : 26, 27	110	— 2 : 2	91	— 3 : 20	94
— 10 : 9	90	— 3 : 13, 15	91		
— 10 : 24	150			II. Peter, generally	138
— 11 : 29	148	I. Thessalonians		— 1 : 21	162
— 12 : 4	135	— 4 : 18	148		
— 13, generally	168			I. John 2 : 19	162
— 13 : 3	90	II. Thessalonians		— 2 : 20	148
— 14 : 3, 19, 34	161	— 1 : 10	146	— 2 : 23	88
— 15 : 12, 21	106	— 2 : 5, 8	103	— 2 : 24	140
— 15, 27, 28	139			— 5 : 7, 8	89
— 15 : 41	161	I. Timothy 2 : 2	148		
— 15 : 44	164	— 2 : 9	148, 149	Jude, generally	138
— 15 : 47	90	— 3 : 13	150	— 11	156
		— 3 : 16	91	— 16	146
II. Corinthians		— 5 : 4	147	— 25	91
— 1 : 3–7	137	— 5 : 22	150		
— 1 : 20	123	— 6 : 25	102	Revelation	
— 2 : 15	142			— 1 : 5	88
— 3 : 3	161	II. Timothy 3 : 16	163	— 1 : 8	91
— 3 : 7	109	— 4 : 7	101	— 1 : 9, 11	94
— 4 : 14	90	— 4 : 14	50	— 2 : 3, 20, 24	94
— 5 : 4	107			— 2 : 25	162
— 5 : 14	129	Hebrews 1 : 4	109	— 3 : 2	91, 94
— 5 : 16	134	— 2 : 3	106	— 4 : 2	83
— 5 : 20	104	— 2 : 8	139	— 5 : 10, 14	94
— 8 : 1	149	— 3 : 11	138	— 15 : 3	94
— 10 : 6	150	— 3 : 16	110	— 16 : 5	94
— 12 : 2	109	— 4 : 2	106	— 17 : 6	135, 146
		— 4 : 3	106, 138	— 17 : 7	135
Galatians, generally	138	— 4 : 4	106	— 17 : 8, 16	94
— 1 : 13, 23, 24	139	— 4 : 6, 7	110	— 18 : 2	94
— 2 : 20	104, 106, 131	— 4 : 8	156	— 21 : 19	102
— 3 : 1	143	— 5 : 1	111	— 22 : 1–5	167
— 4 : 5	109	— 5 : 9	110	— 22 : 14	91, 123
— 4 : 17	146	— 7 : 18, 19	111	— 22 : 18, 19	60

THE END.

www.ingramcontent.com/pod-product-compliance
Lightning Source LLC
Chambersburg PA
CBHW032136160426
43197CB00008B/662